Mayan Mythology

STEPHEN CURRIE

LUCENT BOOKS
A part of Gale, Cengage Learning

 GALE
CENGAGE Learning

Detroit • New York • San Francisco • New Haven, Conn • Waterville, Maine • London

LIBRARY OF CONGRESS CATALOGING-IN-PUBLICATION DATA

Currie, Stephen, 1960-
  Mayan mythology / by Stephen Currie.
    p. cm. -- (Mythology and culture worldwide)
  Includes bibliographical references and index.
  ISBN 978-1-4205-0747-8 (hardcover)
  1. Maya mythology. I. Title.
  F1435.3.R3C87 2012
  398.20897'42--dc23

                                                    2011052629

Lucent Books
27500 Drake Rd.
Farmington Hills, MI 48331

ISBN-13: 978-1-4205-0747-8
ISBN-10: 1-4205-0747-8

Printed in the United States of America
2 3 4 5 6 7 16 15 14 13 12

TABLE OF CONTENTS

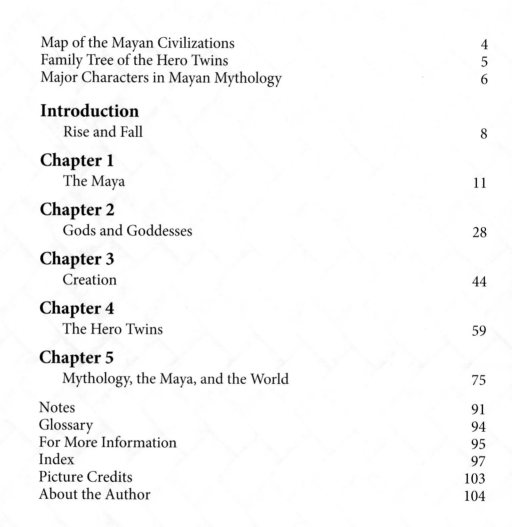

Map of the Mayan Civilizations

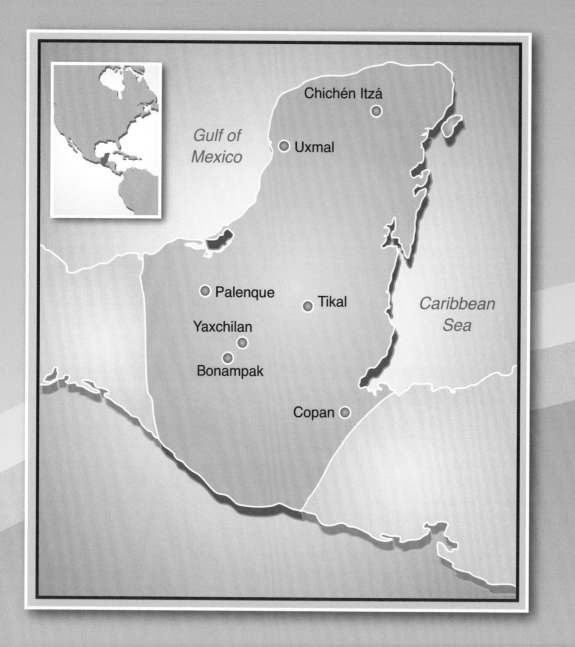

Family Tree of the Hero Twins

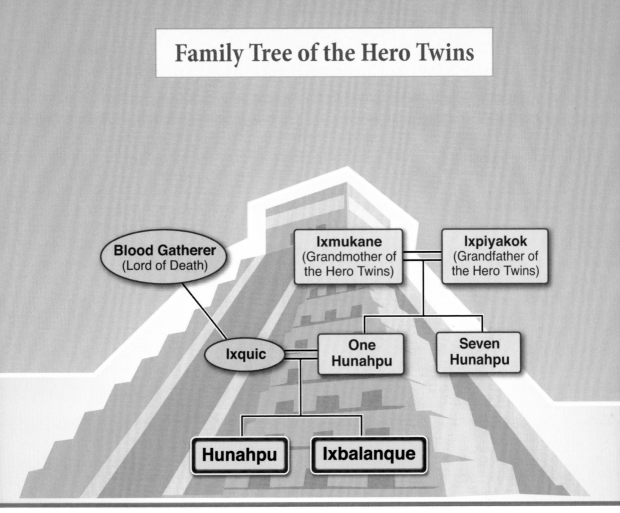

Note: Double lines joining two names indicate that these gods had offspring together. Green shading designates the Hero Twins.

Major Characters in Mayan Mythology

Character Name	Pronunciation	Description
Ah Puch	ah POOCH	God of death.
Alligator		Son of Seven Macaw.
Blood Gatherer		A lord of death, grandfather of the Hero Twins.
Buluc Chabtan	BWAH-luke CHOB-tahn	A god of war.
Camazotz	cah-mah-SOTS	The vampire bat.
Chac	CHOCK	God of rain.
GI'	G I prime	The First Father.
Gugumatz	GOO-goo-mahtz	One of the Makers in the creation story.
Hunahpu	WAHN-uh-puh	One of the Hero Twins.
Itzamna	eet-SAHM-nuh	The most powerful Mayan god, husband of Ix Chel.
Ixbalanque	eesh-bah-lahn-KAY	One of the Hero Twins.
Ix Chel	eesh CHELL	Goddess of the moon and childbirth; wife of Itzamna.
Ixmukane	EESH-moo-cane	Grandmother of the sun; mother of One Hunahpu and Seven Hunahpu.
Ixquic	eesh-KEEK	Mother of the Hero Twins, daughter of Blood Gatherer.
Ix Tab	eesh TOB	Goddess of suicide.
Jaguar Night		One of the first four people.

Jaguar Quitze	**JAG-wahr KEET-say**	One of the first four people.
Kinich Ajaw	**KEE-nitch uh-WAH**	God of the sun.
Kukulcan	**koo-kool-CAHN**	God of the wind.
Lady Beastie		The First Mother.
Majukutaj	**mah-hoo-KOO-tah**	One of the first four people.
One Hunahpu	**One WAHN-uh-puh**	Father of the Hero Twins.
Seven Hunahpu	**Seven WAHN-uh-puh**	Uncle of the Hero Twins, brother of One Hunahpu.
Seven Macaw		An arrogant bird killed by the Hero Twins.
Tepew	**teh-PAH**	One of the Makers in the creation story.
Tojil	**toe-HEEL**	God who brought fire to the Mayans.
True Jaguar		One of the first four people.
Two-his-leg		Son of Seven Macaw.
Yum Kaax	**yoom CAHSH**	Maize god.

Rise and Fall

The words *Maya* and *Mayan* refer to a people from a particular place: the Yucatán Peninsula in what is now eastern Mexico, along with parts of modern-day Guatemala, Belize, and Honduras in Central America. The terms, moreover, are most often used to describe these people during a particular time: the so-called classical era of Mayan civilization, which lasted from about A.D. 250 to 950. During this period the Maya of Central America and the Yucatán established a highly sophisticated urbanized society with a particular emphasis on art, agriculture, and architecture. Along with two other great civilizations, the Inca of Peru and the Aztec of central Mexico, the Maya of this period are generally considered to represent the peak of New World culture before A.D. 1500. Some experts go even further: As one anthropologist writes, the Maya of this time period developed "the finest civilization of Indian America."[1]

The terms *Maya* and *Mayan*, however, also apply to the people of the region who lived before and after the classical period. Indeed, the roots of the classical era lie in developments that took place hundreds of years before A.D. 250. As early as 2000 B.C., for instance, peoples of the Yucatán and Central America were trying new farming methods, ideas that would be refined over the years and would eventually allow the Maya of the classical era to feed hundreds of thousands of people. Similarly, by 300 B.C. the peoples of the region were beginning to develop a detailed calendar and a system of writing, both of which became hallmarks of classical Mayan civilization. The classical period, then, arose from cultural practices that had been developing throughout the area for centuries.

Although the classical era began slowly, it did not end that way. During the A.D. 900s, in the space of just a generation or two, the Maya stopped building cities, lost their position of military and cultural dominance in the region, and allowed the rain forest to take over farmland and temples. No one knows exactly what caused the collapse; theories include environmental degradation, drought, warfare, and overpopulation. There is no questioning the impact on the area and the people, however. According to scholar Michael Coe, the abrupt changes at the end of the Mayan classical era represent "one of the most profound social and demographic catastrophes of all time."[2] Nonetheless, despite the loss of power, wealth, and other features of the classical period, the people who lived in the years following the breakdown maintained many of the traditions of the people who lived during the classical era. Thus, they are considered Maya too.

Several centuries following the collapse, moreover, the situation worsened for the Maya of the region. During the early 1500s, Spanish explorers, soldiers, and priests came to Mayan territory. Before long the Spanish had taken over the entire region, further wiping away the remnants of the classical era. Since the 1500s the region once ruled by Mayan kings has been increasingly influenced by European ideas of government and culture. Nonetheless, experts agree that even today, many of the direct descendants of the Maya of the classical period lead lives that are recognizably Mayan. The Maya of modern times are not in any immediate danger of disappearing. By some estimates, more than half the population of present-day Guatemala is Mayan.

Art, Calendars, and Myths

For most people, though, the classical era is the most intriguing period in Mayan culture. Americans often find themselves drawn toward the romance and mystery of early Mayan civilization. Museum exhibits that display Mayan art and treasures are well attended. Tourists flock to the classical Mayan ruins of Guatemala and the Yucatán, and television stations can count on big audiences for shows about classical Mayan civilization. That interest makes sense because the Maya were distinctive in dozens of ways. They constructed imposing temples and created great stone carvings; they engaged in human sacrifice to appease their gods; they developed an elaborate calendar that governed much of their life and work; they used advanced farming methods to feed an entire civilization on less-than-ideal farmland. The Maya of the classical period, in short, were a compelling people who built a fascinating society.

Of all aspects of Mayan society, none was more distinctive than Mayan mythology. Though the Maya are known in the United States much less for their gods and their myths than they are for their architecture, their writing system, or their fondness for the ritual sacrifice of human beings, the mythology of the Maya nonetheless stands out. Many of the legends and myths of the Maya are good literature. They are well-crafted stories with compelling characters and unexpected plot twists. Some include humor, while others are designed to evoke fear. They are, in short, good stories.

But the myths and legends told among the people of Central America and the Yucatán also have a deeper significance. From tales that tell of the creation of the universe to stories that explain why animals look and act as they do, from narratives in which gods interact with humans to legends that describe the constant battle between good and evil, the mythology of the Maya comes from the depths of the Mayan understanding of the world. Indeed, these stories are uniquely Mayan. They refer to the crops and the animals known to the Maya, they are set in landscapes remarkably like the ones where the Maya lived, and they address themes of joy, sadness, and struggle that would have been familiar to any Maya of the classical era. Mayan mythology sprang from the truths of Mayan life—and in turn shaped what the Maya did and thought. In every way, the myths and legends of the Maya reflect the experience of being Mayan.

CHAPTER 1

The Maya

From A.D. 250 until the 900s, during the classical period of Mayan culture, the Maya were the dominant civilization in Central America—and the most highly advanced in the entire New World. Expert astronomers, farmers, and artists, the Maya developed a rich and compelling way of life. Among many other achievements, the Maya invented a system of writing, constructed elaborate pyramids and urban centers, and designed a complex and accurate calendar. Though the Maya occupied only a relatively small section of the Americas, Mayan cultural, artistic, and religious influences spread well beyond their territory. Indeed, the Maya are justly remembered today as one of the great civilizations of their time.

Mayan Religion

Of all the noteworthy aspects of Mayan culture, Mayan religious beliefs and practices were among the most distinctive and absorbing. Mayan religion included a dizzying array of gods, rituals, stories, and more. From the burials of kings to tales of heroic twins, from blood-spilling ceremonies to sacred animals, the Mayan religious world was everywhere. Indeed, religion made up the foundation of much of Mayan

The Maya saw the universe as divided into three parts: the earth at the center, the sky above, and the underworld below.

society. The Maya used religion to help them make sense of the world—and as a means to influence the world to work in their favor. In every way, religion was at the heart of what it meant to be a Maya.

The Mayan worldview, which underlay most of the Mayan religious beliefs, was complex. According to Mayan tradition, the universe was divided into three interrelated parts. At the center was the earth, which was viewed as the back of an enormous turtle or crocodile. Flat and shaped like a circle, the earth was divided into five regions, representing the four basic directions—north, south, east, and west—and the center of the circle. The Maya symbolized the various regions with bird species, types of trees, and most of all with colors: red for east, yellow for south, blue for west, and white for north.

The central region was especially important to the Maya, and the tree that symbolized this region was of particular significance. Far larger than the trees that represented the four outer sections of the earth, the central tree was known as Wacah Chan, or World Tree. Wacah Chan was not only big; it was also the point at which the earth was most closely connected to the rest of the universe. Like a pencil sticking vertically through a flat cardboard disk, Wacah Chan stretched both up above the earth and down below it. Its trunk and branches reached high into the sky, the second section of the universe, and its roots extended deep into the underworld, the universe's third and most mysterious sector.

The Sky and the Underworld

In the Mayan worldview, both the sky and the underworld were of major importance. Like the earth, each was symbolized by an animal: the sky with a two-headed dragon, the underworld with the belly of a crocodile. To the Maya, the sky was an arch consisting of thirteen layers, each rising farther away from the surface of the earth. Every star and planet belonged to a particular layer, and each of these celestial bodies was believed to move back and forth within that layer as it traveled through the sky. The tallest branches of Wacah Chan reached through all of these layers, too, eventually coming to an end in the thirteenth and highest layer of the heavens.

Just as the Mayan sky consisted of layers moving progressively farther from the earth, so too did several layers make up Xibalba, the Mayan underworld. And just as Wacah Chan's highest branches reached the topmost layer of the sky, its deepest roots likewise extended down to the lowest level of Xibalba. Still, Xibalba was not simply a mirror image of the sky. Whereas the sky had thirteen layers, the underworld had only nine. And in contrast to the sky, which contained little more than celestial bodies and the homes of a few gods, Xibalba was a vibrant place. As archaeologists Linda Schele and David Freidel write, "Xibalba had animals, plants, inhabitants of various kinds, and a landscape with both natural and constructed features."[3]

A *Star Wars* Extra

A brief scene in the 1977 movie *Star Wars* (now known as *Star Wars IV: A New Hope*) was filmed among the ruins of the Mayan city Tikal.

Xibalba was also central to Mayan religious thought. The Maya imagined the underworld to be populated by a group of deities known as the Lords of Xibalba, or the Lords of Death. These divinities were lethal. "Xikiripat and Kuchamakik' made people vomit blood," one myth notes. "Ajalmes and Ajaltoq'ob' caused heart attacks and sudden death."[4] Not surprisingly, living Maya generally avoided Xibalba. Nonetheless, Mayan tradition tells of a road running to Xibalba from the surface of the earth, and some stories report that this road was traveled by a few brave Maya in the early days of the world. Indeed, Mayan tradition holds that several cave systems in and around the Yucatán mark the beginning of this road.

Worship

As the stories about the lords of Xibalba suggest, the Maya were polytheistic; that is, instead of believing in just one deity—as is the case with Islam, Christianity, and Judaism, to name a few modern faiths—the Maya, like the Greeks and Romans, believed in many different gods and goddesses. Each of these divinities had his or her particular interest and sphere of influence. The goddess Ix Chel, for example, was in charge of childbirth; the god Xaman Ek, who was associated with the North Star, helped protect travelers. Other deities were connected with rainfall, crop growth, the wind, and so on. To the Maya, the gods were all-powerful. "Collectively," writes anthropologist John Henderson, "they [held] sway over human affairs."[5]

With every part of the Mayan world governed by one or more deities, the Maya often tried to influence these gods and goddesses to act in their favor. Prayer was one means of accomplishing this. "Great lord of the sky who art placed in the clouds," ran one Mayan prayer to the sun god, "give us a good year of [crops]."[6] Making paintings, figurines, and other images of the divinities was another way to gain their favor. Sometimes images and prayer were combined. One early Spanish account mentions that pilgrims often traveled to the Mexican island of Cozumel, where they prayed to a statue of Ix Chel. The Spanish did not show much respect for the Mayan beliefs—"The unhappy dupes believed the idol

spoke to them,"[7] the writer observed with deep scorn—but the Maya accepted that these prayers were the best way to earn the goddess's support.

Most often, however, the Maya sought to influence the gods and goddesses through religious ceremonies. On certain days of the Mayan year, for example, adult Maya were expected to fast as part of religious observances. On other days, the Maya kindled special fires, made offerings of food to the gods, or took part in sacred dances. As the Maya saw it, the gods demanded these rituals in exchange for extending their good will. By taking part in these and dozens of other rites and ceremonies, the Maya believed they were pleasing the gods and keeping themselves in the deities' good graces.

A fresco depicts Ix Chel, the goddess of childbirth. The Maya believed in many different deities, each with his or her own specific area of interest or influence.

The Mayan Calendar and the End of the World

The Maya are perhaps best known today for their elaborate calendar. One of the most accurately produced by any society before the modern era, this calendar included several different repeating cycles. One of these cycles had 20 days, each one with its own name. This cycle meshed with a separate cycle in which each day had a number from 1 to 13. The first day of this joint sequence was 1 Imix: day 1 in the numbered system and the day called Imix in the named system. There were 260 separate dates in this cycle; once all 260 had been used, the sequence began again.

That was not the only system used by the Maya to keep track of time, however. Another parallel system consisted of years of 365 days, divided into eighteen months of 20 days each, with 5 days left over at the end. In this way, each day of the year had two different designations: a number-name designation and a month-day designation. Combining these two systems produced a unique identifier for each day in a fifty-two-year period. The Maya then grouped the fifty-two-year units into even larger units, some of them (called the Long Count) including more than five thousand years apiece.

The precision of the Mayan calendar makes it possible to plot the endpoints of these units into the future and the past. One of these endpoints appears in the present day: December 21, 2012. Some recent writers have suggested that the end of the Long Count is always associated with major changes in the universe, such as natural disasters, and many of these have argued that the 2012 date marks the end of the world. Though this idea has gained notice in popular culture, serious scholars have demonstrated that any link between 2012 and the end of a Mayan calendar cycle is purely coincidental.

A Mayan calendar made of stone shows separate cycles of twenty and thirteen days.

Bloodletting

By modern standards, many of these sacred ceremonies seem unremarkable. Fasting, for example, plays a role in many religions today, and sacred dances are common as well. Other Mayan ceremonies, however, have little connection to mainstream religious practices of today. In particular, the Maya had many rituals in which participants deliberately cut themselves to draw blood. "Self-mutilation was carried out," writes Coe, "by jabbing needles and stingray spines through ears, cheeks, [and] lips . . . the blood being spattered on paper or used to anoint idols."[8] One well-known Mayan carving shows a queen pulling a thorny vine through her tongue.

These bloodletting rituals had several meanings. Kings spilled their blood to allow deities to enter their bodies, thus connecting the king more firmly to the divine. Kings and queens also bled themselves in order to celebrate their relationships to their ancestors; in Mayan religion, royal blood quite literally connected kings and queens to the past. But perhaps most importantly, according to Mayan tradition, the gods required human blood to stay alive. As a result, the Maya frequently engaged in rituals that involved blood. As religious scholar David Carrasco writes, "Bloodletting was done at the dedication of buildings and monuments, the birth of children, marriage ceremonies, all political events, moments of transition in the calendar, and at life cycle rituals."[9]

While many Mayan rituals required only a small amount of blood, others called for much more blood than one person—or even several people—could safely provide. In these situations, it was impractical for queens and kings to supply the blood themselves; the amount needed would quickly kill them. As a consequence, the Maya frequently engaged in human sacrifice, or the ceremonial killing of people. Most often their victims were drawn from the ranks of prisoners of war, but in some circumstances the Maya sacrificed adults and children alike from their own communities.

Sometimes death came quickly to the victims of human sacrifice. In these instances, the victim was beheaded, or the

A stone relief depicts a Mayan queen pulling a thorny vine through her tongue in a bloodletting ritual, which was a common part of religious ceremonies.

heart was cut out with several well-placed strokes of a blade. "Four old men . . . held the arms and legs of the victim," writes Coe, describing one common method of carrying out a human sacrifice, "while the [chest] was opened up by another individual."[10] In other cases, however, the victim's death was slow. A religious leader made multiple cuts on the victim's body, making the victim bleed to death—a process that could take hours. However the blood was obtained, the ceremony was usually carried out in public; the Maya believed that the gods preferred it that way.

Though obtaining blood was usually the most important part of human sacrifice, some victims were sacrificed for other purposes. One early European account of Mayan culture, written by Spanish bishop Diego de Landa, notes that a certain well was frequently used for sacrifice. "Into this well they . . . had the custom of throwing men alive as a sacrifice to the gods, in times of drought,"[11] Landa reported. Archaeological evidence supports Landa's account. In addition to typical sacrificial offerings such as bowls, incense burners, tools, and precious stones, the well contains the bones of men, women, and children sacrificed over several centuries as an offering to the rain gods.

Royalty

As implied by the importance of royal bloodletting, Mayan kings and queens were seen as more than just men and women; instead, they were sacred beings who could channel the divine, and their consciousness could travel into other worlds. For instance, although Xibalba was off-limits to living Maya, the kings and queens could enter the underworld through the power of the mind. To accomplish this, they put themselves into a religious frenzy that involved calling on—and sometimes channeling—the spirits who lived in the underworld. Xibalba, write Schele and Freidel, was "the parallel unseen Otherworld into which the Maya kings . . . could pass in ecstatic trance."[12]

Following their deaths, moreover, Mayan kings and queens were believed to make an actual journey to Xibalba. This was a necessary step in their quest to become gods themselves. Though the way was long, tradition held that the more important royals reached this destination. Once there, they could eventually be transformed into deities and move on to a new home in the heavens. To assist in the process, the Maya buried their leaders with objects designed to encourage the gods to look favorably upon them. The tomb of a Mayan king

Translation Please

In the early 1960s, American scholar Tatiana Proskouriakoff successfully deciphered the Mayan writing system. For the first time, modern experts were able to read inscriptions and other texts from the Mayan classical period.

Art and Religion

During the thousand or more years since the heyday of the Maya, much of the artwork of the classical period has disappeared. That is particularly true of anything created on perishable materials, notably paper and cloth, which degrade quickly in the hot, humid climate of Central America. "Every temple, every palace room, was probably festooned with curtains and wall hangings," writes Michael D. Coe. "Virtually all of this has disappeared without a trace in the tropical environment." Even sturdier artworks have suffered. Stone carvings have worn down in the rain and wind. Murals have faded; figurines have broken beyond recognition.

The art that does remain from the classical period, however, shows a close connection between the art of the Maya and their religion. Many of these artworks, though not all, reflect the spiritual practices and the religious beliefs of the Mayan people. Dozens of surviving figurines, for instances, depict gods and goddesses. Similarly, stone carvings often show quetzals, jaguars, or other animals sacred to the Maya, and murals sometimes picture kings, queens, and ordinary citizens engaged in worship. All of these examples make it clear that the art of the Mayan people often flowed directly from their religious experiences.

Michael D. Coe. *The Maya.* New York: Thames and Hudson, 2011, p. 104.

A figurine wears a quetzal feather headdress and jaguar skin, items from animals that were sacred to the Mayan people.

known as Pacal or Hanab Pakal, for instance, contained not only his body, but pottery, carvings, and other artworks. The lid of the king's sarcophagus, or casket, was especially impressive; it included representations of dragons, jewels, birds, and Pacal's ancestors, along with symbols representing the Mayan underworld. "The intricately carved sarcophagus lid," Carrasco writes, "depicted the image of the Maya cosmos and Pacal's movement through it."[13]

Human sacrifice also played a role in getting rulers to Xibalba. In Mayan tradition, the souls of commoners could assist kings in completing the journey from the grave to Xibalba. Accordingly, leaders were often buried with the bodies of prisoners or ordinary citizens. These people were sacrificed specifically so they could help the rulers find their way to the underworld. As the Maya saw it, the lives of commoners and captives were less important than the goal of getting a dead ruler to Xibalba. As with the carvings on Pacal's sarcophagus, the human sacrifices represented the unshakable belief of the Maya that their kings and queens could attain full divinity after their deaths.

Mayan kings and queens also took pains to emphasize their godlike qualities while still on earth. Through dress, actions, and ritual, rulers encouraged their people to see them as incarnations of the gods—that is, as the gods in human form. In particular, they frequently wore and carried objects associated with a specific god. The king of a Mayan region called Dos Pilas, for example, often wore belts, animal heads, and other symbols linked to a god of war. As Carrasco puts it, "Once arrayed with these prestigious and potent objects, [the kings] hardly appeared human at all." Instead, Carrasco writes, "these royal persons were living cosmograms [representations of sacred objects] designed to inspire awe, respect, and obedience."[14]

Mayan art often emphasized the connection between the kings and the gods as well. Many Mayan artworks depict rulers in poses or in clothing that suggests that the king was divine. A stone carving from a Mayan city-state called Kaminaljuyu in modern-day Guatemala, for example, shows a king dressed as a bird god. Just as important as his costume, though, is his position in the artwork: He is floating above the earth, approximately halfway to the top of the sky. The placement indicates that the king should not be viewed as strictly human. Rather, as a museum exhibit on Mayan kingship notes, "the Kaminaljuyu lord is portrayed as the universal bridge between the heavens and the earth."[15]

The members of Mayan royal families had temporal, or worldly, duties in addition to their responsibilities as religious figures. The Maya had no strong central authority, so the Yucatán and nearby parts of Central America were divided into dozens of kingdoms or city-states, each with its own ruling family. "With the advice of his ruling family and council," Carrasco writes, "[the king] directed the work of intensive agriculture and trading, initiated the outbreak of conflicts with other communities, and regulated the rewards for the maintenance of social status."[16] Still, it is impossible to separate the political responsibilities of the royal families from their religious obligations. Every Mayan ruler was at once a governor, a judge, and a military commander—as well as a sacred figure to his or her people.

Warriors, Artisans, and Scribes

Given their importance to both government and religion, it is no surprise that the royal families were at the top of the Mayan social system. These people were wealthy, educated, and politically powerful. The richest among them lived in luxury, in conditions that almost any European ruler of the time would have coveted. One three-story palace in the city of Cancuen, for example, had 270,000 square feet (25,084 sq. m) of floor space. And tomb excavations make it clear that even in death the kings were showered with goods and treasures that the ordinary Mayan family could never have afforded.

Though ruling families had the highest social status among the Maya, other social classes ranked nearly as high. Mayan warriors were one example. Mayan city-states often warred with one another or with outsiders, and the men who fought these battles were much admired. Indeed, many Mayan artworks highlight and glorify soldiers. Scribes were another high-status group. To keep records of tax payments, astronomical observations, and other important matters, the Maya developed a writing system that used glyphs, or simple pictures, to stand for syllables, sounds, and objects. Using these glyphs, scribes carved inscriptions into stone and produced books made of bark. The Maya

prized these writings, and they prized the scribes who did the writing, too.

Artisans were yet another respected class within Mayan society. Some Mayan artists carved intricate designs into stone, many of them representing gods or other religious figures. Sculptors carved jade into elaborate figurines of warriors, gods, and kings; potters fashioned cooking vessels, containers, and other everyday items from stone and clay. Other artists painted murals on the walls of temples. More than any other American culture—and more than many civilizations of Asia and Europe as well—the Maya are associated with sophisticated artistic techniques and ideas. As art historian Mary Ellen Miller puts it, "In its complexity and

A fresco depicts a Mayan warrior. Both warriors and artists were highly respected in Mayan society.

subtlety, in its sheer volume and innovation, Maya art is the greatest of New World art styles."[17]

Mayan architecture, too, is highly regarded by modern observers. Coe's book *The Maya*, for example, uses the words "awe-inspiring," "magnificent," "perfect," and "wonderful"[18]— all on a single page—to describe Mayan buildings. The centers of urban areas typically featured temples—many of them in the shape of pyramids—palaces, and plazas, often connected by a series of stone passageways and staircases. These city centers were ambitious: The tallest of the Mayan pyramids, Temple IV in the city of Tikal, rises to a height of about 220 feet (67m). The resulting cities served the Maya well, too. The largest urban areas may have had over a hundred thousand inhabitants. Certainly Mayan cities were the most impressive and sophisticated in the New World of their time.

Laborers and Farmers

The bulk of Mayan society was made up not of kings, warriors, and artisans, but instead of laborers and farmers who made up the lower classes—the poor of the Mayan city-

Several classes of Mayan society are depicted in a pyramid according to status, with royalty at the top and farmers and laborers at the bottom.

states. By some estimates, about 90 percent of all Maya were members of this social class. These people provided the labor to build palaces, temples, and roads. Their main responsibility, however, was farming. Mayan farmers grew a variety of crops, including avocados, papayas, chili peppers, squash, and beans. The most important crop by a considerable margin, though, was maize, or corn. Supplemented by fruits and other vegetables, along with the meat of native animals such as deer, maize was present in one way or another at nearly every Mayan meal.

Where maize was concerned, the Maya were expert farmers. Because much of the region was filled with thick underbrush and tall trees, Mayan farmers began by burning a stretch of forest to produce a milpa, or a field suitable for agriculture. Once the ashes had cooled, farmers used a pointed length of wood called a digging stick to help them plant their crop. As Henderson describes the process, the farmer "ha[d] only to poke holes in the ash with his digging stick, drop in the seeds . . . and wait for the rain."[19] Throughout the summer the maize would grow steadily, assuming all went well. Four or five months after the planting, the crop would be ready to be harvested.

Farming Challenges

Unfortunately for the Maya, there were two significant obstacles to producing a good crop. The first was soil. In much of Mayan territory, the soil is scarcely thick enough to cover the underlying rocks. As an early Spanish visitor to Mexico noted, "Yucatán is the country with the least earth that I have seen, since all of it is one living rock and has wonderfully little earth."[20] Moreover, the soils of Central America and the Yucatán are not especially rich or fertile. A Mayan milpa often produced just two or three seasons' worth of maize before its nutrients were used up. Worse yet, the soil was extremely slow to rejuvenate. Once a milpa was depleted, it had to lie fallow for up to twenty years before it could support another set of crops.

Although the quality of the soil presented difficulties for Mayan agriculture, rainfall was perhaps an even bigger concern. Though in most years rainfall was sufficient to produce a good crop, the rains were not consistent. When

Fateful First Contact

The first contact between the Spanish and the native people of the Yucatán took place in 1511. In 1527 Spain launched its first major military campaign in the region, and by 1546 the Spanish had conquered all of the peninsula.

rainfall totals were significantly below average, crops failed, with disastrous consequences. On multiple occasions throughout Mayan history, drought brought widespread famine to the Mayan people. Indeed, many archaeologists believe that a period of sustained drought during the 800s and 900s was the major factor in bringing the classical era to an end.

Drought was a special concern for the Maya because they did not have much recourse when droughts came. Other early civilizations diverted the flow of rivers or dammed up lakes to bring surface water to their crops, but the Mayan homelands had few lakes and few large rivers. As for underground resources, in most parts of Mayan territory water not only lay hundreds of feet below the surface of the earth but was separated from the surface by thick layers of rock as well. Although the Maya used natural sinkholes and constructed wells to collect water for drinking or cooking, they could not tap nearly enough groundwater to make up for a year of below-average rainfall. And while the Maya often traded with their neighbors, an exceptionally dry year caused such widespread suffering that trading for food could not alleviate the situation.

Over the years, drought led to thousands upon thousands of deaths from starvation among the Maya. But in some ways the mere threat of drought was just as alarming. Farmers went into each wet season hoping that rainfall would prove sufficient to produce a good crop—but knowing that no matter how hard they worked, no matter how well-timed their planting, all their labor and ingenuity would be useless if the rains failed to come. Since the farmers themselves could not make it rain, they hoped that the gods who made and guided the world could do so—and would, moreover, if the Maya could only keep the gods happy. Like many other peoples throughout the ages, the Maya turned to religion to help them control that which they could not control themselves.

This, then, was the culture that produced the mythology of the Maya. Agricultural yet urban, artistic yet violent, encouraging creativity yet preoccupied with death, Mayan society encompassed a wide variety of values and beliefs. Like Mayan religion, the myths and legends of the Maya are firmly rooted within this culture. From creation stories to morality tales, from gods to heroes and villains, Mayan myths spring from the realities of life in Central America and reflect the goals and ideals of Mayan society. Like the myths and legends of other peoples throughout time, the myths of the Maya can be fully understood only within the context of the culture that produced them.

CHAPTER 2

Gods and Goddesses

T hough many Mayan myths tell of human beings, animals, and other mortal creatures, the central figures of Mayan myths and legends are divine. Indeed, gods and goddesses are everywhere in Mayan mythology. Some rule the stars, govern the winds, or control the rains. Others take on the form of birds, disguise themselves as the sun or the moon, or bring death to unsuspecting people on earth. In addition to these duties and responsibilities, the gods and goddesses in the Mayan tradition have their own personalities and life stories as well. Some are kind, others cruel; some are ugly, others beautiful. Whatever their characteristics, the most important Mayan gods and goddesses are often distinctive and always intriguing.

Questions and Ambiguities

Given the Mayan focus on religion, it would be reasonable to assume that modern archaeologists and anthropologists have learned nearly everything important about Mayan gods and goddesses. That assumption, however, would be incorrect. In fact, there are many gaps in our understanding of the Mayan deities. Even the number of gods and goddesses is unknown. One count dating from the 1700s listed 166 different deities;

later researchers, however, suggest that the actual total may be considerably higher. Some modern scholars have given up any attempt to count them. Coe, for example, sidesteps the question entirely. The Maya, he writes, had a "bewildering number of gods."[21]

One reason for the confusion is that individual gods often had more than one persona. Many Mayan deities appeared in multiple forms, often with different names and characteristics. A god might adopt one persona when he appeared in the northern quadrant, for example, while becoming something quite different in the west. Similarly, some deities sometimes manifested themselves as male and sometimes as female, while others switched between being good and evil or shifted their appearance from animal to human. No one really knows whether the Frog God, the God of Unlucky Days, and

A clay figurine represents the Mayan goddess of beekeeping, one of several deities that some scholars believe was manifested in several different ways in the culture's mythology.

Beware of the Owl

The Mayans considered owls, bats, and dogs to be symbols of evil. Some of the most malevolent gods were often pictured together with one or more of these animals.

the Mistress of the Bees, among many other divinities mentioned occasionally in Mayan sources, are separate entities or simply manifestations of some other, more powerful deity.

Moreover, information about Mayan deities is often lacking or ambiguous. Similar-looking glyphs from different Mayan sources may refer to the same god—or to two completely different deities. Names of gods did not necessarily remain consistent through time or from one part of the Mayan world to another. And translators who wrote the names of the gods in their own language did not always hear the names the same way or use the same letters to represent the sounds. The name of the Mayan sun god, for instance, appears in different books today as Ah Kin, Kinich Ajaw, and Kitix, among many other variations. Determining which god is which, therefore, is a complicated task.

Still, although much about the Mayan gods and goddesses remains uncertain, archaeologists have substantially improved their knowledge of Mayan deities during the past half century. By studying inscriptions on walls and stone tablets, examining glyphs in the few books that survive from the classical era, and collecting stories from modern-day Maya, experts have developed an increasingly complete understanding of who the Mayan gods and goddesses were and what they did. To be sure, questions remain, but their number is decreasing. Today, archaeologists and other researchers can speak with confidence about the major gods of the Mayan tradition—and about many of the less important gods as well.

Itzamna

The most powerful of the Mayan gods was a deity named Itzamna, also spelled Itzam Na or Itzamnaaj. This god, whose name literally translates to "lizard house," was sometimes known as "the god of all."[22] In carvings, paintings, and other artworks, Itzamna was occasionally portrayed as an iguana. More often, however, he is shown in human form. In these latter pieces of art, Itzamna was depicted as an old man in a seated or squatting position. These pictures generally show him with a hooked nose, an elaborate headdress, and a distinguished bearing. Images like these strongly suggest the importance of Itzamna.

Of all the gods in Mayan mythology, Itzamna may well have been the wisest. Certainly he was the most interested in learning and culture. In Henderson's words, Itzamna was celebrated as a "patron of knowledge";[23] part of Itzamna's role was to educate the Maya and to help them make sense of their world. Indeed, the Maya of the classical era credited Itzamna with having invented the Mayan writing system, as well as their complex calendar. According to the legends, Itzamna demanded nothing from the Maya in return for these two great gifts. It was a sign of Itzamna's benevolence and love for his people that he had freely given his inventions to the Maya to use as they saw fit.

A corner of a structure in the Temple of Frescoes depicts a stucco mask of Itzamna, the most powerful of the Mayan deities.

In addition to his benevolence and his wisdom, Itzamna was also unusually powerful. Though many Mayan gods had the ability to change themselves into different forms, Itzamna outdid them all. He frequently appeared in the guise of a lizard, for example, but could also turn into a tree, a rock, or a bird. Several other gods, notably Itzam Cab, a god of fire, were widely believed to be manifestations of Itzamna, too. In addition, Itzamna could take on the guise of a fellow god—and, if he liked, he could take over that god's duties as well. As author and artist Leonard Everett Fisher puts it, "Itzamna could become anything or anyone he wanted to be."[24] To the Maya, Itzamna's ability to change his appearance and identity was nothing short of remarkable.

For some Maya, in fact, Itzamna's powers and abilities made it almost unnecessary for other gods to exist. If Itzamna could take the place of the rain god, the sun god, or any other god he chose, then there was little reason to pay much attention to other deities. Indeed, there is evidence that Itzamna's overwhelming powers moved some people to reject all divinities besides him. As archaeologist J. Eric S. Thompson writes, "It rather looks as though the Maya of the Classic period had developed the cult of Itzam Na into something close to monotheism"[25]—the belief that there is just one god. From this perspective, Thompson notes, other divine beings were different forms of Itzamna, not separate gods at all.

In accordance with his power and high status, Itzamna was frequently featured in Mayan art. During the classical period, for example, Mayan workers carved dozens of images of Itzamna into the walls of the House of Masks, a palace in the city of Kabah. These carvings may have indicated that the builders were hoping to receive special favors from Itzamna, or they may simply have signaled the sacredness of the site. Certainly the carvings suggested that Itzamna might be found in or near the building. "Buildings guarded by Itzamna were places of divination [prophecy] and priestly power," write archaeologists Linda Schele and Peter Mathews. "The House of Masks . . . proclaimed its potency with its dazzling façade."[26]

Despite Itzamna's strengths and his benevolence, though, not all Maya found him equally compelling. Evidence suggests that Itzamna was primarily a god of the upper classes

Of Gods and Kings

In Mayan art, the sun god Kinich Ajaw is usually portrayed with two distinguishing features: squarish, squinting eyes, and a single large front tooth shaped like an uppercase letter *T*. Not only did these features made Kinich Ajaw easy to recognize, but the tooth, in particular, served as a convenient shorthand for the god. Just as the letter *M*, when written in a certain color and shape, identifies a McDonald's restaurant today, so too could a Mayan artist suggest Kinich Ajaw just by drawing that easily recognizable tooth.

During the classical era, several Mayan rulers had their own front teeth filed into the form of a T. In part, they did this as a way of seeking Kinich Ajaw's favor. They hoped Kinich Ajaw would interpret their actions as an offering to him; if so, he might be grateful and feel honored, which would make him more likely to act on the kings' behalf. For a society that believed that the gods required constant praise and thanks, this perspective made a great deal of sense.

At the same time, though, the kings had a second goal in mind: They hoped

to associate themselves with Kinich Ajaw in their people's minds. They wanted to imply that they were not just kings, but divinities—earthly manifestations of the powerful sun lord. This ruse often lasted past the ruler's lifetime. When a powerful Mayan king named Hanab Pakal died, for example, his heirs buried him in a mask that matched the sun god's face, including especially the oddly shaped tooth. "With the T-shaped tooth," Mary Ellen Miller writes, "the dead, masked Hanab Pakal must have taken on . . . the guise of the Sun God . . . forever young and firm of face, even though he was a man of eighty years of age."

Mary Ellen Miller. *Maya Art and Architecture*. New York: Thames and Hudson, 1999, p. 75.

Hanab Pakal's death mask includes a T-shaped tooth in tribute to the sun god.

rather than of the peasants. Though the lower classes during the classical period certainly recognized him as a deity, Itzamna appealed more to Mayan nobles and ruling families. Perhaps this was in part because of Itzamna's connection with knowledge and learning. The upper classes, after all, were literate and trained in the intricacies of the calendar, while the peasants were not. Whatever the reason, with the collapse of the classical era and the corresponding decline of the upper classes, Itzamna became an afterthought at best. "Itzam Na is completely absent from present-day peasant rites in Yucatan,"[27] Thompson points out.

Ix Chel

If Itzamna was the most important god in Mayan mythology, then his wife was no doubt the most important goddess. Known today by various names, including Ix Chel, Lady Rainbow, Chak Chel, and Goddess Q, Itzamna's wife was not nearly as powerful as her husband; still, she had impressive powers. Moreover, Ix Chel sometimes matched Itzamna in kindness and in care toward her people. Indeed, one of Ix Chel's most important roles was as goddess of the moon. Some Mayan legends describe how Ix Chel would take on that role when Itzamna became the god of the sun. When these two supreme deities played these parts, they helped keep the world in balance and brought comfort to their people below.

Ix Chel had other positive characteristics, too. Most notably, she was the goddess of childbirth. By asking Ix Chel's favor, pregnant women believed they could increase their chances of having a safe delivery and producing a healthy baby. Ix Chel was also strongly associated with medicine, and people sought her approval when epidemics broke out. "The priests," wrote Landa, describing a ceremony in a town where sickness had taken root, "brought out their medicine bundles in which they carried around . . . various little idols of the goddess of medicine, Ix Chel."[28] Other gods and goddesses were involved with healing, too, but if Ix Chel, the wife of the powerful Itzamna, could not help a person who was ill, it was not clear whether any other deity could be of assistance.

Like her husband, Ix Chel also took an interest in knowledge and learning. In particular, the Maya credited Ix Chel with having invented weaving. "Because [Ix Chel] was the first person on earth to weave," writes one commentator, "she was deemed patroness of the art of weaving."[29] Moreover, again like her husband, Ix Chel taught this new process to her people, enabling them to make clothing and other fabrics. Even today, it is common for Mayan women of Guatemala and the Yucatán to make an offering to Ix Chel before beginning a new weaving project.

Ix Chel had a darker side, however. From time to time the Maya were hit by devastating floods, which destroyed crops and swept away homes and villages; the worst of these floods killed hundreds of people as well. Ix Chel was widely believed to be responsible for the flooding, and most Mayan legends claim that she purposely brought the floods upon her people. This explanation is echoed by pictures and figurines of Ix Chel that show her as an ugly, formidable warrior brandishing a weapon. Other images of Ix Chel are even less flattering: Some portray her, in Coe's words, "with snakes in her hair and . . . claws [on] her feet and hands."[30] Both poses suggest evil; certainly, neither is at all pleasant to see.

A terra-cotta figurine depicts a Mayan weaver. The goddess Ix Chel was said to have taught the Mayans the art of weaving.

The Sun and the Rain

While Itzamna often took on the role of the sun god, Mayan legends generally agree that there was a separate sun god as well. Known as Kinich Ajaw, among countless other variations, this god was believed to be nearly as powerful and kind as Itzamna himself. "He was a friendly god," writes Fisher, "who brought good health and happiness to his people."[31] Like countless other peoples throughout time, the Maya much preferred the light of day to the darkness of night. In their view, the night was peopled with enemies, malevolent spirits, and dangerous animals. The day, in contrast, was safe; the Maya's enemies retreated, and the warmth and light from Kinich Ajaw enabled the people to grow crops and see the world around them.

Like Ix Chel, however, Kinich Ajaw was not always a sympathetic figure. His nighttime activities, for example, were problematic. In Mayan legend Kinich Ajaw traveled to the underworld each evening at sunset and spent the nights in Xibalba in the form of a jaguar. He returned each morning on schedule, but the Maya sometimes worried that he would fail to return, having decided instead to cast his lot with the evil lords who ruled Xibalba. Moreover, although the Maya appreciated and honored the sunlight that Kinich Ajaw brought them, they were aware that too much sun would bring drought. As religion scholar Michael Kampen writes, "The Maya knew . . . that his gaze could scorch their tender maize plants and cast famine over their lands."[32] Because of Kinich Ajaw's role in bringing drought, the Maya did not necessarily trust him as they trusted Itzamna.

Although the Maya routinely invoked Kinich Ajaw's name when drought threatened their livelihoods, another god was believed to be more responsible for the withering of crops. That god was Chac, the god of rain. Since Mayan society relied so heavily on agriculture, and since agriculture in turn was dependent on appropriate levels of rainfall, Chac took on an importance that went well beyond his actual

Chaos Contained

Toltex was the Mayan god of chaos. He originally lived in the sky with many of the other gods. But according to legend, when he tried to bring chaos to the earth, the other gods forced him to live in Xibalba.

A figurine depicts Chac, the Mayan god of rain, who was particularly important to a society dependent upon agriculture. Modern farmers still call upon Chac for help during times of drought.

powers. "For the ordinary Maya farmer whose paramount interest was his maize field, Chac was the all-important deity," point out authors Robert J. Sharer and Sylvanus Griswold Morley. "His friendly intervention was sought more frequently than that of all the other gods combined."[33]

Like most other Mayan gods, Chac had multiple manifestations. Indeed, he was often thought of as four related deities, each connected to a particular point on the compass. To the east, for example, Chac was known as Chac Xib Chac, or the Red Chac of the East. To the south, in contrast, Chac appeared in yellow and was called Kan Xib Chac. Whereas the Maya believed that several other gods also changed personas based on geography, they emphasized this feature for Chac in a way that they did not for most other gods. This emphasis was not accidental. By ensuring that each compass direction had its own manifestation of Chac, Fisher writes, "Chac could protect every part of the land of the Maya—not one area would be overlooked."[34]

The importance of Chac to the Maya, moreover, has been especially long lasting. During the six or seven centuries of the classical era, some gods—even important ones—came and went, or changed characteristics over time. Many gods who were worshipped throughout these years rapidly declined in popularity once the classical period was over; Itzamna is a good example. In contrast, researchers believe that the Maya have worshipped Chac for over two thousand years. Not only was Chac an important god long before the classical era began, he remains a respected figure even today. "Modern Christian Mayan farmers still recite prayers to the rain god Xib Chac in times of drought,"[35] writes scholar C. Scott Littleton.

In Mayan art, Chac typically had the body of an elderly man. His face, however, bore a closer resemblance to the face of a reptile or amphibian rather than a human being. Among other features, for example, Chac was usually portrayed with fangs. Beyond these basics, Chac was portrayed in a variety of ways, depending on what aspect of Chac the artist wished to emphasize. At times he was shown shedding tears, for instance, which Mayan scholars believe to be a symbol for rainfall. Alternatively, Chac was shown carrying objects that could be used to create thunder and lightning. These objects included serpents, conch shells, and more. "In case anyone doubted his power," writes author Anne Rockwell in a retelling of a myth about Chac, "he would hurl his ax across the sky to make lightning and beat his drum to make thunder."[36]

The Wind and the Corn

Closely associated with Chac was the god of the wind, sometimes known as Kukulcan. Indeed, Chac and Kukulcan are so tightly associated in Mayan legend that some scholars

Ix Chel and Floods

Virtually all Mayan legends agree that the deity who caused flooding was Ix Chel. A few myths, however, reject the notion that Ix Chel caused the floods out of malice. In these versions, Ix Chel was not cruel at heart; neither did she bring about the floods as punishment for something the Maya had done—or failed to do. Instead, these stories assert that the flooding was accidental. Moreover, according to these myths the floods came out of something good: Ix Chel's love for her husband.

These myths reference the widespread Mayan belief that Itzamna, Ix Chel's husband, often took on the role of the sun god. According to legend, on these occasions he transformed himself into the sun and traveled through the skies. When he became the sun, however, he left his wife behind in the home they shared. As these stories describe it, Ix Chel became lonely when her husband was away. Hoping to spend more time with him, she routinely transformed herself into the moon and dashed around behind him in an attempt to get as close to him as possible.

The moon, however, is the major influence that causes tidal changes. It exerts a gravitational pull on the earth, pulling water in various directions as it moves and making the tides move in and out. The result of Ix Chel's constant motion was perhaps predictable. "As she chased after him," one writer explains, "the tides would rise, creating floods that inundated the fields and caused the crops to die. So enamored was she, that Ix-Chel did not even notice the havoc she was causing." It was love, not anger, then, that caused the floods.

Todotulum.com. "Posada Yum Kin Hotel." www.todotulum.com/travel-guide-yum-kin-185.html.

argue that the wind god is simply one more representation of Chac and not a separate deity at all. Others point out strong similarities between Kukulcan and the Aztec god Quetzal-coatl, although, again, whether they are identical is unclear. Kukulcan appears in most Mayan artworks as a serpent with feathers. His mouth is shaped like the bill of a duck, and his breath is most often visible as it comes out of his mouth—a way of symbolizing the wind.

In Mayan lore, Kukulcan and Chac worked together to bring the needed rains to Mayan farmers. First, Kukulcan brought moisture into the sky and blew it toward Chac. Then Chac would transform the moisture into rain. Helping to provide rain, however, was not Kukulcan's only responsibility. Among other duties, for example, Kukulcan served as a patron of the ruling families. And as was true with other Mayan gods, some members of these families sought to

A sculpture of Kukulcan, the Mayan god of wind, depicts him as a serpent with a mouth shaped like a duck's bill.

associate themselves as closely as possible with Kukulcan by dressing in clothing that resembled his. In Kukulcan's case, unfortunately, this led to complications for later researchers. "At least one prominent historical personage . . . bore [Kukulcan's] name as a title," writes Henderson. "Traditional histories confuse this man . . . who became a larger-than-life cultural hero, with the god."[37]

The maize god, sometimes called Yum Kaax, was another god whose favor the Maya sought out. Yum Kaax was responsible for giving farmers the seed they needed to grow their crops. He was also in charge of protecting the plants as they grew. Not as powerful as Chac, Yum Kaax was usually portrayed as a young man. His face was strikingly handsome, his hands swayed like a cornstalk moving in the breeze, and his hair was as long and straight as the silk on an ear of corn. The overall effect was one of balance and beauty. As Miller writes, "The Maya Maize God embodied human perfection."[38] By portraying Yum Kaax in this flattering way, the Maya hoped to sway him to support the farmers' efforts.

Malevolent Forces

For the most part, the gods described above were benevolent. Though they could and did act in damaging or destructive ways—as demonstrated, for instance, by the flooding caused by Ix Chel or by Chac's occasional refusal to provide life-giving rains—these deities did not dislike the Maya or wish to harm them. According to legend, these gods and goddesses generally wanted to do what their people requested. As the Maya saw it, a few sincere prayers, a carving or painting of the god in question, or a ceremony involving human sacrifice usually sufficed to win the favor of a divinity such as Yum Kaax, Ix Chel, or Itzamna.

Not all the gods and goddesses of Mayan legend were so well-disposed toward their people, however. Nor were they all so easily approachable. On the contrary, several of the Mayan deities were unpleasant, cruel, or downright murderous. A few of them, indeed, personified evil. These gods and goddesses were widely feared by the Maya and were avoided whenever possible. Ah Puch, a god of death, was one example. Ah Puch "stalked people," writes Fisher, "especially the injured, looking for an opportunity to take them from this world."[39] It is no surprise that Ah Puch was most often pictured in the form of a skeleton with a grim and mocking smile.

The Maya also attributed evil actions and thoughts to their gods of war. These gods were called upon when kingdoms fought one another, of course, as well as when non-Mayan enemies attacked. Though some of these divinities had good points—one was a special protector of merchants, for example, in addition to his duties as a war god—they were for the most part bloodthirsty and cruel. According to Sharer and Morley, the war god Buluc Chabtan "is often shown burning houses with a torch in one hand while he demolishes them with a spear in the other."[40] As long as gods such as Buluc Chabtan only attacked the Maya's enemies, such belligerence was acceptable. Still, at any moment it was possible that the gods of war could turn on their own people—with potentially disastrous results.

Other gods were likewise associated with death, pain, and malice. Most of these were at least as unpleasant as Ah Puch or Buluc Chabtan. Ix Tab was the goddess of suicide; Mayan artists most often showed her dead, with a cord wrapped around her neck, and surrounded her with symbols of death. The various gods associated with the planet Venus were believed to be evil-minded and treacherous. A violent god known as Zotzilaha Chimalman, one source reports, "dwelt in the House of Bats, a gruesome cavern on the way to the abodes of darkness and death."[41] And at least one deity was even more appalling than Ix Tab, Zotzilaha Chimalman, or any of the Mayan war gods. "There is no benevolent side to Manik, the god of human sacrifice,"[42] Fisher writes flatly.

Gods and the World

To the Maya, then, the world of the gods and goddesses could be either comforting or alarming. For every benevolent god, such as the supreme deity Itzamna, there was a cruel and violent god, like Manik, the deity of human sacrifice. For every god who could be won over with simple expressions of prayer, there was another who demanded death in exchange for his or her help and attention. Indeed, the Mayan deities quite often combined good and evil within the same figure. For every vicious war god who sometimes showed unexpected patience and generosity toward his people, there was a deity such as Ix Chel, who sometimes interrupted her duties as healer and weaver to bring dreadful floods to the Maya who worshipped her.

This double-edged view of the gods, in which some were good, others were evil, and still others were both, matched the way the Maya viewed the world around them. On one level, the Maya loved their homeland. In a good year, it produced excellent corn crops—enough to feed millions of people in a relatively small geographic area. During the classical era in particular, the Maya were blessed with great material wealth, enabling them to develop a way of life that emphasized learning, art, and other cultural riches. And yet the world was never reliably safe. Droughts came and went. Floods wiped out entire crops, causing starvation and panic. Warfare was rampant; society was highly stratified. The world of the Maya, in short, was both good and evil. It is no surprise that the Mayan gods and goddesses were depicted likewise.

Strange Names, Indeed

Some Mayan gods are best known today by the names given to them during the classical era. Others are better known by names given to them by scholars who came much later. These include the Principal Bird Deity, the Tonsured Maize God, and God N, among many others.

CHAPTER 3

Creation

The myths developed and told by cultures around the world always include creation stories—narratives that tell how the world came to be. Besides describing how the earth, animals, and human beings appeared, creation stories spring from the realities of the culture that produces them. By emphasizing certain characters in the narrative or by ordering the events of the creation as they do, creation stories point to the needs, values, and dreams of the society that made them. At the same time, creation stories also help shape the culture. As mythology expert David Adams Leeming writes, "The creation myth serves as a model for everything we do . . . the creating of a family, the destroying of what we do not like, the building of a house, the planting of a field, the making of a work of art."[43] In this way, the Mayan creation stories are central to the Maya's concept of themselves.

Different Stories

The Maya have a number of different creation stories. One of these narratives, for example, explains that the world was created and destroyed eight times before the rise of human beings. In this account, which appears on a set of panels at a temple in the city of Palenque, the first god was a being known as the First Father to the Maya—and as GI' to the archaeologists who found and translated the panels. The myth explains that GI' appeared on earth in 3122 B.C., toward the end of the eighth version of the world. One year later, GI' was joined by the First Mother, who was also known by the delightful name of Lady Beastie.

In 3114 B.C. a new creation began. Though everything else was destroyed, GI' and Lady Beastie took on the responsibility of moving the new creation from chaos to order. "1 year, 9 months, and 2 days after the new epoch began," the Palenque panels explain, "GI' entered the sky."[44] From this vantage point, the First Father divided the earth into sections according to compass bearings, and gave the sun, the moon, and the stars their current positions and cycles. The First Father also set up the World Tree at the center of the earth. Over the next several hundred years, moreover, GI' and Lady Beastie became the parents of many children, some of whom became gods and others of whom became kings and lords on earth.

A panel found in the temple ruins at Palenque conveys a version of the Mayan creation myth alongside a depiction of the transfer of power from a king to his son.

This creation story has several important themes. Of these, perhaps the most significant is the ordering of the universe. The narrative emphasizes that the universe replaced chaos. In this way the legend assures the Maya that even when the events of the universe may seem random, the world does in fact have a purpose and an organizing principle. The account emphasizes the primary place of the gods, too. The chronology, in particular, establishes the legitimacy of the First Mother and Father. The narrative explains that these two figures date back to before the creation that resulted in the current universe. As Linda Schele and David Freidel point out, "Their power comes from a time before the existence of our world."[45]

Another creation story, this one associated with an archaeological site in present-day Guatemala, also mentions First Father's ascent into the sky; however, this version goes further by explaining that First Father was the creation of two other deities known as the paddler gods. These gods were believed to paddle each night across the sky in a cosmic canoe. "On the night of 4 Ahaw 8 Kumk'u," or August 13, as the legend describes it, "the paddler gods made the image of . . . three stones appear."[46] The stones were hearthstones, symbolic of a cooking fire, which in turn symbolized both destruction and birth. The image of the hearthstones called First Father into being. According to the tradition, this creation took place in the constellation of Orion, not on earth, and First Father took shape from the shell of a tortoise. Like the story from Palenque, this Guatemalan version emphasizes that the gods come from a period before the current world was created.

The Popol Vuh

Though these and other creation stories appear within the Mayan tradition, the best-known version of the creation saga comes from a book called the Popol Vuh. Sometimes referred to as the Book of Counsel or the Mayan Bible, the Popol Vuh is an important sourcebook of Mayan mythology, and much of the volume deals with the story of creation. The creation story as it appears in the Popol Vuh is by far the most complete and detailed of all surviving versions of the Mayan creation legend. Indeed, when Mayan scholars speak

The Popol Vuh

The Popol Vuh is the best single source of information on the Maya and their mythology. At the same time, the book is not entirely a primary source. That is, it does not come directly from the classical era of Mayan civilization. Instead, the book has a long and complicated history. It came into being in 1558, just a few decades after the arrival of the Spanish, when an unknown Mayan decided to write down some of the stories that were most central to his people's traditions. (He may have used an earlier book written in Mayan glyphs as a source, but if he did, that book no longer exists.) That man had learned to read and write using Spanish letters, and he used these letters to approximate the sounds of his Mayan language.

This version of the Popol Vuh attracted little notice at this point. In 1701, however, a Roman Catholic priest found the 1558 manuscript tucked away in a church in Guatemala. He translated the document into Spanish. The Popol Vuh disappeared from view for another century and a half after that until another cleric discovered the translation in a Central American library, brought it to Europe, and translated it into French. Later, other scholars translated it into English and other languages as well, and knowledge—and appreciation—of the Popol Vuh extended across the world. Its original Mayan author could scarcely have imagined the fame of his book today.

of the Mayan creation myth, they frequently mean the myth that appears in the Popol Vuh.

The creation story in the Popol Vuh begins with a nearly empty world. As anthropologist and author Victor Montejo writes in his retelling of the story, "There were no people, no animals, no birds, fish, crabs, rocks, ravines, no mountains."[47] Dennis Tedlock, another translator of the original book, puts it perhaps even more poetically: "Whatever there is that might be is simply not there."[48] At this stage, the Popol Vuh explains, the world had just two features. One was an endless sky, empty of stars, planets, and other celestial bodies. The other was a motionless sea, devoid of waves, tides, or marine life. The world was without sound, without light, and without activity.

Even at that early stage, however, the universe did contain several deities. Some of these divinities lived in the sky. Among these was a powerful god known as Tepew, or Heart of Sky, who was in charge of lightning and fire. Other gods and goddesses made their homes in the sea, where, despite the general nothingness, they were surrounded by the blue-green feathers of the quetzal, a bird of special importance to the Maya. Among these gods was Gugumatz, also known as Heart of Earth or the Great Feathered Serpent. Similar in looks and actions to Kukulcan, the god of the wind, Gugumatz also had much in common with the Mayan supreme god, Itzamna; some scholars suggest that Gugumatz is simply a manifestation of one of these two divinities.

As the Popol Vuh tells it, Gugumatz and Tepew decided to create a more interesting world. "Let it be this way," the two gods resolved after some discussion. "The water should be removed, emptied out for the formation of earth's own plate and platform."[49] Through their magical powers, Gugumatz and Tepew instantly caused land to appear where formerly there had been nothing but sea. Next, they added contours to the land, creating hills, valleys, and mountains. In turn, lakes and rivers appeared among the hills and valleys. Finally, the two gods filled the land with trees, flowers, and other plant life. The earth as the Maya knew it was in place.

"Creatures in the Trees and Forests"

The creator gods, sometimes known as the Makers, were delighted with their work at first. As they saw it, the newly formed earth represented perfection. Soon, however, they grew dissatisfied. In part, the problem was the quiet and the lack of movement in the world they had made. "Will there be only silence and stillness beneath the tree branches and vines?" Gugumatz and Tepew asked themselves. Beautiful as it was, the world was soundless, sterile, and uninteresting. The solution to this concern was clear. "It would be good if there were creatures in the trees and forests,"[50] the Makers told each other, and they set out to make new beings to populate the earth.

The Makers had a second reason for wanting creatures in the universe. Pleased as they were with their accomplishments, they realized they wanted more than just valleys and islands: They wanted glory. Unfortunately, at this stage of the creation it was impossible for them to receive the attention they coveted. Trees and rivers could not offer praise to the gods. Neither could vines or mountains show gratitude to the Makers. To get the tribute and recognition they desired, the gods needed intelligent beings on the earth—beings that could of their own free will name and glorify the gods who had made them and all the earth around them. The Makers' new goal, then, was to create beings that were expressive, aware, and articulate.

They began by creating the wild animals native to the rain forest, seacoast, and meadows of the Yucatán and Central America. In an instant the earth came alive with pumas, snakes, and dozens of other species. The Makers sent each animal to a different spot and designed each creature for success in its environment. Deer, for example, were sent to live in clearings and by the banks of the rivers. Birds, similarly,

The Creation of Earth, *by Mexican painter Diego Rivera, depicts the Mayan creation myth as told in the Popol Vuh.*

were given wings and assigned to build nests in the trees, while jaguars were predators who roamed across the forest floor. Together, the animals were given dominion over the earth and everything in it.

Initially, this stage of creation once again appeared to be a triumph. The world became a more active, more exciting place as it filled with animals. But the success proved illusory. When the Makers commanded the animals to speak the names of their creators, the animals could not. "They just squawked, they just chattered, they just howled,"[51] the Popol Vuh explains. The Makers did not have the ability to make the animals any more responsive or eloquent than they already were. Accordingly, they allowed the animals to keep their bodies and their homes, but stripped them of their right to govern the earth. Instead, the animals would serve a new and higher form of life. "From now on," Tepew and Gugumatz informed the animals, "your flesh will be consumed and eaten. This is your fate."[52]

People of Mud, People of Wood

The Makers next set themselves the task of building a more intelligent creature. "How else can we be invoked and remembered on the face of the earth?"[53] they asked themselves, justifying their decision. This time, they used mud and clay to sculpt a human body. Once again, though, they were disappointed with the results. The mud was soft and squishy, so the body failed to hold its shape, especially when it rained. And although the human could speak, its words were gibberish. "It spoke as one with its face in the ground," writes Deborah Nourse Lattimore in her retelling of the tale. All it could say, she explains, was "Mlax-akx-blux."[54] Neither did the clay person have any feelings or any understanding of the world. Clearly, this was a failed experiment, and the Makers destroyed the man of clay.

Next, the Makers made people out of wood. The results this time were much more successful; as Tedlock writes, the new creatures were "manikins, woodcarvings, human in looks and human in speech."[55] The wooden beings could not only put together coherent sentences, but they could also produce offspring, and they could move without fear that their bodies would fall apart. Unfortunately, the wooden people's bodies were twisted and weak, and they had neither blood nor flesh. Nor did they have feelings or souls. "These ignorant beings burned the bottoms of their cooking pots," the Popol

Aztec and Mayan Mythologies

Before the arrival of the Europeans in the early 1500s, there were two great civilizations in what is now Mexico. One was the Mayan. The other was the Aztec, who were based in present-day Mexico City, west of the territory of the Maya. Although the classical era of Mayan civilization had ended long before the corresponding high point in Aztec history—the Aztec Empire was close to the height of its political power and cultural influence when the Spanish reached the Americas—the two traditions nonetheless have much in common.

Their myths show several of the connections between the Maya of the classical era and the Aztec many centuries later. Both the Aztec and the Maya worshipped dozens of gods, each of which was responsible for a particular aspect of the world; in each culture, moreover, overlapping names, manifestations, and duties make it difficult to determine how many distinct gods the society actually had. In some cases, there are clear parallels between a deity in one culture and a deity in the other. The Mayan wind god Kukulcan, for instance, has many of the same characteristics as the Aztec deity Quet-

zalcoatl. The creation myths of the two cultures show some points in common as well. In Aztec mythology, for instance, the world was destroyed by a massive flood at one point during the creation process; this flood, of course, is reminiscent of the rising waters that wiped out the wooden people in the Mayan Popol Vuh. Similarly, creation myths of both the Aztec and the Maya explain that monkeys are examples of failed human beings.

The Aztec deity Quetzalcoatl shares characteristics with the Mayan god Kukulcan.

The Gods' Flesh and Blood

According to one version of the Mayan creation myth, the first truly human people were not made out of corn. Instead, the gods cut off their fingers and let them fall to the ground, where they turned into people. Fortunately for the gods, the fingers grew back.

Vuh reports, "and beat and starved their dogs."[56] Worst of all, the wooden people were unable to praise their creators. Once again, they were not what the Makers intended.

This time the gods punished the wooden people for failing to offer proper thanks and praise to the Makers. Jaguars tore the wooden figures open and crushed their bones. Vultures flew down from the skies and pecked out their eyes. Camazotz, the vampire bat, ripped their heads off their bodies. The wooden people's dogs crushed their masters' faces as payback for the abuse and neglect they had suffered, and the cooking pots, likewise seeking revenge, threw heated rocks at the wooden figures. Grinding stones completed the job by crushing the wooden figures into bits. "[The wooden people] were pounded down to the . . . tendons," writes Tedlock, "smashed and pulverized even to the bones."[57]

Just in case any of the wooden people survived this hideous treatment, the gods had another penalty in store: a massive flood designed to sweep all the wooden people off the face of the earth. Thanks to the rising waters and the concerted effort of inanimate objects, the gods very nearly succeeded in wiping out the wooden people. "[The wooden people] tried to climb onto the house tops, but the roofs collapsed and flung them to the ground," Montejo writes. "They even tried to hide in caves, but the caves blocked off their entrances so that they couldn't get inside."[58] In the end, with their shelters unavailable, practically all of the remaining wooden people drowned. The handful that survived, according to Mayan legend, became the ancestors of today's monkeys—an animal, the Popol Vuh points out, that looks and acts much like a person, yet has no soul, no speech, and no human understanding.

The Corn People

Though frustrated by this latest failure, the Makers continued to attempt to create human beings who would give them the homage they felt they deserved. Since mud and wood had been ineffective, they cast around for a new material. They soon learned that four animals—a fox, a coyote, a parrot, and a crow—had discovered a spot called Bitter Water Place, where maize grew abundantly. Recognizing the importance of corn as a potential staple crop for the humans that were to come, Gugumatz, Tepew, and the other Makers chose maize as a raw material for creating intelligent, aware human beings with souls.

The Makers traveled to Bitter Water Place. They used corncobs to make the bodies of four men, and pounded corn kernels into meal to construct the men's arms and legs. Ixmukane, the grandmother of the sun, then ground more corn to provide muscles and power to the men. Next,

A mural by Mexican painter Castro Pacheco is based on an element of the Mayan creation myth that tells of man being created out of ears of corn.

she mixed water with still more corn to make fat, filling out the people and giving them bulk. The Makers named the first four men Jaguar Quitze, Jaguar Night, Majukutaj, and True Jaguar. "No woman gave birth to them," the Popol Vuh emphasizes. Yet these four men were quite definitely human. As one translation puts it, "People they came to be. They were able to speak and converse. They were able to look and listen. They were able to walk and hold things with their hands."[59]

At last, the Makers believed, their efforts had been crowned with success. They checked to make sure that everything about the four men was perfect—and indeed it was. The men could not only speak but they spoke sensibly. Their hearing was outstanding, and their vision was even more impressive. The men made of corn could see through any obstacle—rocks, trees, mountains, and more. More remarkable still, they could see all the way to the end of the earth without any loss of clarity. Just as was true of the gods, nothing could happen on the face of the earth without the four maize men knowing about it.

"They Are Not Gods"

The corn people were properly appreciative of the gifts they had received. When they thanked the gods for bringing them to life and offering them understanding and knowledge, however, the Makers grew nervous. The corn men, they decided, were entirely too smart and articulate. Nor had the Makers intended the new human beings to have such powerful eyesight. The gods suspected that humans with these godlike talents might eventually stop praising the Makers who had created them. But the corn people were not intended to be deities, nor were they supposed to think of themselves in that light. "They cannot possess our powers," the Makers told each other, worried. "They are not gods like us [who can] see everything clearly in the sky and on the earth."[60]

To fix the problem, the Makers threw fog into the eyes of the corn people. This action permanently clouded the corn people's vision. While the new humans could see things that were nearby, just as humans can do today, they were no longer able to see through solid objects or look across the entire world. The fog also entered the new humans' minds, interfering with their knowledge and understanding of the world. By fogging the corn people's eyes and brains, then, the gods made the new creatures less than perfect—and kept them in a subservient relationship to the deities.

The Makers were not quite finished. As the four corn men slept, the gods fashioned four corn women, one for each of the men. The four couples recognized the power of the Makers and acknowledged the work the gods had done to create them. The eight men and women gathered in the darkness on top of a hill near Bitter Water Place, and recited a prayer imploring the gods for protection, health, and children. "Do not forsake us!" the prayer read in part. "Let us be fruitful and multiply. Give us many level and safe fields and let our people have much peace and happiness."[61] The prayers were successful. Each couple soon had children, who spread out across Central America and the Yucatán and in turn had children of their own. Before long, according to legend, these original four couples had given rise to all the different Mayan peoples.

Meaning and Significance

On one level, like all creation legends, the Mayan creation myth is simply a tool that explains how the world came to be and tells why the world is structured in certain ways. The Mayan creation story, for example, explains why human beings outrank animals and are allowed to eat their flesh. It also accounts for the fact that animals cannot speak, and it details why monkeys look somewhat—but not exactly—like people. Similarly, by describing how the original four couples each founded a number of Mayan tribes, the story clarifies how there came to be so many different groups of Maya. The myth even explains why people cannot see around solid objects or to the ends of the earth. Explanations like these are quite common in creation stories from around the globe.

Powerful Paper

The phrase Popol Vuh comes from two Mayan words, *pop* and *vuh*. *Vuh* means paper. *Pop* literally translates to straw mat, but symbolizes power.

More significant, though, the Mayan creation story helps explain what it means to be Mayan. The creation myth as described in the Popol Vuh strongly reflects Mayan culture and its values. Most notably, maize held a place of extreme importance within Mayan society. As the crop most often

A sculpture of the Mayan god of corn, shows him wearing a crown made of corn cobs. A staple of the Mayan diet, corn plays a prominent role in the culture's creation story.

planted and eaten by the Maya, it provided many of the nutrients that kept the Maya alive. Indeed, when maize did not grow, the people starved. It is no surprise, then, that according to the Mayan creation story, the original humans were formed from corn. To the Mayan people, maize was metaphorically the foundation of life. In the creation legend, maize was quite literally the stuff from which life was formed.

The story of the founding of the different tribes also demonstrates the importance of the creation story in Mayan culture. Though many of the Mayan tribes had similar ways of life, they differed in many respects. Mayan peoples spoke a variety of languages, and they had no strong central government to bind the groups together politically. Their skin colors varied, as did their facial features and their styles of dress. Yet despite the linguistic, political, and other differences from one group to the next, each tribe saw itself as part of a larger group: as one community among many peoples who all proudly referred to themselves as Maya. By describing how the first four couples gave rise to all the Mayan peoples, the creation legend encouraged a sense of connection among all the tribes.

Another meaning of the myth involves the role of prayer and appeals to the gods in Mayan life. The narrative makes it clear that the gods react with disappointment or anger when their creations do not worship them properly. When it becomes evident that the animals cannot speak, for example, the Makers demote them; when the wooden people do not recognize the powers that gave them life, the gods destroy them. In a sense, the Mayan creation story serves as a cautionary tale. It is a reminder to Maya to keep their gods firmly in mind, praying to them often and making offerings of praise and thanks. Otherwise, the story implies, the gods could take revenge on their people just as they did on the animals and the people of mud and wood.

The Mayan account of creation as told in the Popol Vuh, then, is more than just a good story. On the contrary, it serves as a mirror of Mayan society and a guide to what the Maya believed was important. From demonstrating the importance of corn in Mayan culture to explaining how it could be that so many disparate groups were all Maya, the creation myth of the Popol Vuh shows what the Maya value. Likewise, by describing why it was acceptable to eat animal flesh and by underscoring why the Maya should pray, the creation saga explains why the Maya behave as they do. The Mayan creation myth provides a window into Mayan culture. It reveals, in short, the Maya's own image of their society and shows modern readers what being a Maya was all about.

CHAPTER 4

The Hero Twins

Myths and legends from across the world often describe battles between the forces of good and the forces of evil. The heroes and villains in these stories are most commonly humans—though humans who are gifted with unusual strength, intelligence, or other powers. The struggles between these forces are titanic and often come to involve the entire world. The story usually involves physical fighting but may also include battles of will or of the mind. Tales about the clash between good and evil often climax with the death of one or more of the characters, too, though in the magical world of legends and myths, of course, there is no guarantee that any dead body will actually stay that way.

In any culture, the tales of heroes and villains are among the most memorable and most celebrated of all myths and stories, and Mayan mythology is no exception. Indeed, the struggle between good and evil forms the heart of one of the most compelling of all Mayan legends—the story of how two brothers, Hunahpu and Ixbalanque, triumphed over the mighty Lords of Death. Like the Mayan creation story, the saga of Hunahpu and Ixbalanque—often called the Hero Twins—is enjoyable in its own right. It is well known, and rightly so, for its strong depiction of characters, its occasional touches of humor, and its sprawling plotline, which carries the story across two generations. But again, like the creation story, the story of the Hero Twins is also interesting for what it reveals about the Maya, their culture, and their perspective on the world around them.

One Hunahpu and Seven Hunahpu

The tale of the Hero Twins is complex. In addition to including disguises, a variety of characters, and a sometimes convoluted series of events, the story encompasses two different time periods—the first of which takes place long before the Hero Twins were born. Indeed, although the saga begins with a birth, it is not the birth of the heroic brothers Hunahpu and Ixbalanque but the birth instead of two other boys, One Hunahpu and Seven Hunahpu. To make matters even more confusing, One Hunahpu and Seven Hunahpu were twins themselves, and these two boys would eventually become the father and uncle, respectively, of the Hero Twins.

One Hunahpu and Seven Hunahpu, the original set of twins in this myth, came from an important lineage. They were the sons of Ixpiyakok and Ixmukane, an elderly god and goddess; Ixmukane, the grandmother of the sun, was the woman who helped create the corn people by grinding maize to make their muscles and fat. As was appropriate for the sons of two respected deities, the boys were widely believed to be representatives of good. "They are great thinkers and great is their knowledge," reads Dennis Tedlock's translation of the story. "There is only good in their being and their birthright."[62]

From early on, the boys had one great interest: a ball game known as pokatok, which was in fact an extremely popular sport among the Maya. Played on I-shaped courts inside large open-air arenas, pokatok required a rubber ball and two opposing players or teams. The stakes were often high: Whereas the Maya celebrated the winners of an important pokatok game and treated them like

American Pokatok League

Some Americans have recently developed a sport called the Modern Royal Ballgame, which is loosely based on pokatok as it might have been played in Central America. In February 2011 a Modern Royal Ballgame tournament was held in Pasadena, California.

kings, the losers were humiliated and—according to tradition, at least—sometimes paid for the loss with their lives. As the story tells it, both One Hunahpu and Seven Hunahpu quickly became expert pokatok players. They won every match they played, and they practiced their skills whenever they could.

Unfortunately for the twins, the court where they practiced and played was directly above Xibalba, the underworld of Mayan legend. Xibalba was a dangerous place. It was ruled by the magical kings known as the Lords of Xibalba, or the Lords of Death, and these rulers were as evil as the twins were good. Whenever possible, the lords brought havoc, death, and destruction to the earth above them. Some caused people to bleed. Others made them vomit. Even the names of the Lords of Xibalba reflected their ugly personalities: The list of lords includes such unappealing names as Pus Master, Skull Scepter, and Blood Gatherer.

The ancient Mayans enjoyed watching and playing the sport of pokatok, a ball game played in open-air courts.

To Xibalba

Offending the Lords of Xibalba was unwise, but the twins managed to do exactly that. The Lords of Death could hear One Hunahpu and Seven Hunahpu playing pokatok, and the constant banging of the ball on the court filled them with rage. Moreover, the lords interpreted the fact that the boys were playing ball within earshot of Xibalba as a sign of deep disrespect. "They have simply failed to honor us," one of the lords complained. "Certainly they act arrogantly here over our heads."[63] The lords decided to summon the boys to Xibalba by challenging them to a game of pokatok. Once the twins were in the underworld, they reasoned, they could punish the boys and, if they chose to do so, kill them.

Young and confident, the twins underestimated the threat posed by the Lords of Death. Believing that they could easily defeat the lords at pokatok, One Hunahpu and Seven Hunahpu accepted the challenge and headed toward Xibalba; however, the path was more difficult than they thought. First, they had to descend a sheer cliff. Then they needed to cross the River of Churning Spikes. The spikes threatened to cut them to pieces, and the boys barely managed to reach the other side safely. Next came two more rivers, one flowing with blood and the other with pus. "They crossed," the Popol Vuh comments wryly, "but did not drink."[64] Once again, the twins had avoided harm.

The twins soon arrived at Xibalba, where they were met with ridicule and humiliation. Instead of greeting the twins in person, the lords had made life-sized puppets of themselves and set them on a bench. Fooled by the realistic figures, the brothers tried to begin a conversation with the puppets, whereupon the lords appeared and laughed loudly at the twins' stupidity. Next, the lords encouraged the twins to sit down—on what turned out to be a superheated rock. The brothers "got up fast," Tedlock writes, "having burned their butts." The Lords of Death laughed even louder at the success of this second prank. As Tedlock translates it, "The laughter rose up like a serpent in their very cores."[65]

The lords then ushered the boys to a place called the Dark House. They were shut inside a room, where each was given a torch and a cigar and told to light both. The brothers would not be allowed to extinguish the flames, the lords explained, but they would need to give the cigars and torches back the next day in the same condition as they had received them. One Hunahpu and Seven Hunahpu could see no way of complying with these instructions. By morning the cigars

Pokatok

According to archaeological evidence, pokatok was unquestionably the primary sport of the Mayan people. Most large towns had at least one pokatok court; some had several. The largest known court discovered thus far, at the Chichén Itzá site in the Yucatán Peninsula, was about 550 feet (168m) long—about 150 feet (46m) longer than the standard dimensions of a Major League Baseball stadium, measured from home plate to the center field fence, and almost twice as long as a standard field used for soccer or football.

More than that, however, pokatok was an important part of Mayan culture. Games between top teams or players were major events that attracted thousands of spectators. Gamblers placed wagers on the outcomes of important matches, and skilled players were highly respected. And pokatok games were a frequent feature in Mayan art and literature. Murals and carvings often show pokatok games in progress, for example, and the best-known stories in Mayan mythology also refer to pokatok games.

In the opinions of many experts, the connections between pokatok and culture go even further. "Symbolically," write mythology experts Ann Bingham and Jeremy Roberts, "the ball represented the Sun, Moon, or planets, and the court represented the cosmos." In this way, the ballplaying skills of both sets of twins are related to the deep regard for astronomy that distinguished Mayan society. Similarly, the game of pokatok was a handy metaphor for warfare and for life and death. Authors Linda Schele and David Freidel, among others, suggest that when Mayan kings played pokatok, they may have been deliberately trying to link themselves with the Hero Twins.

Ann Bingham and Jeremy Roberts. *South and Meso-American Mythology A to Z*. New York: Chelsea House, 2010, p. 14.

An athlete in traditional dress plays the ancient game of pokatok.

and torches were nearly burned up. The twins had failed the test, and so the Lords of Xibalba put them to death. Before burying their bodies, they cut off One Hunahpu's head and mounted it in the fork of a dead tree by the side of a road.

Pregnancy and Birth

The battle involving the twins seemed to be over. Killed by the more clever Lords of Death, they had evidently lost the struggle. But in fact the story had only just begun. When the Lords of Xibalba placed One Hunahpu's head in the dead tree, the tree immediately came back to life and began to grow fruit. Word of this remarkable tree began to spread. Among those who came to see the spectacle was a young Xibalban named Ixquic. Ixquic was the daughter of Blood Gatherer, a lord of the underworld. When she attempted to pick one of the fruits, One Hunahpu's head spat into her hand. The saliva made Ixquic pregnant. Though One Hunahpu and his brother were dead, their lineage would live on.

Blood Gatherer soon discovered that his daughter was pregnant. Enraged, he summoned his owls—birds associated with death in the Mayan tradition—and ordered them to take Ixquic away and kill her. He also instructed the owls to bring Ixquic's heart back to him as proof that she was dead. Ixquic, however, convinced the owls that the death sentence was unjust. She collected red sap from a nearby tree and let it harden. The result looked and felt like a human heart. Then Ixquic gave the owls the dried sap to bring to her father. The Lords of Xibalba gleefully burned the sap, believing that it was actually Ixquic's heart. "In this way, the lords of Xibalba were defeated by a maiden," Tedlock writes, "all of them were blinded."[66]

The Stars Are Born

In some versions of the Hero Twins legend, the four hundred boys killed by Seven Macaw's son Alligator ascend into the sky and become the stars.

Meanwhile, Ixquic made her escape by climbing from Xibalba up to the surface of the earth. She sought out Ixmukane, the mother of One Hunahpu and Seven Hunahpu, and explained that she was carrying One Hunahpu's child. Ixmukane was not sure at first whether to believe Ixquic, and she was of course distraught at the news that her

sons were dead. In the end, though, Ixquic remained with Ixmukane until her child was born. Both women were surprised, however, when Ixquic delivered not one baby, but two: twin sons named Hunahpu and Ixbalanque. The children of Ixquic and One Hunahpu, these two boys became the Hero Twins.

Seven Macaw and His Sons

From the very beginning, Hunahpu and Ixbalanque were destined for greatness. "The main task of the Hero Twins was to rid the world of anomalies [things that are not normal] and monsters,"[67] writes Coe. Their first conflict was with a vain and evil-minded bird called Seven Macaw. Seven Macaw had eyes and teeth that were made of jewels and reflected light in all directions. Because of this, Seven Macaw believed that he was the sun. He viewed himself as the most important being in all creation, and his constant boasting became an irritant to the creatures of the world. Seven Macaw's boasts became so annoying, in fact, that the Hero Twins decided to kill him.

When Seven Macaw came to feed on the fruit of a tree, Hunahpu used a blowgun to shoot the bird. The shot broke

According to Mayan myth, the Hero Twins were conceived when One Hunahpu's head spat into the hand of Ixquic, the daughter of one of the Lords of Death.

Seven Macaw's jaw and badly damaged his eyes and teeth, but did not kill him. Furious, the bird attacked the twins, bit off Hunahpu's arm, and flew home with it. Eager for revenge—and of course the return of Hunahpu's arm—the twins got an old man to pretend to be a great healer who could repair jaws and eyes. Seven Macaw begged for the man's assistance in fixing his face. But the twins had the man replace the bird's remaining jewels with maize kernels instead. "Robbed of his source of conceit and vanity," writes author Michael Schuman, "Seven Macaw no longer had any reason to live, and he keeled over and died."[68] Hunahpu retrieved his arm from Seven Macaw's house and reattached it easily.

Next, the twins set out to kill Seven Macaw's sons, Alligator and Two-his-leg. Both sons were enormous, boastful, and powerful. Alligator had killed four hundred boys by dropping a house on their heads; Two-his-leg bragged that if he stamped his foot the hills would crumble. The twins began by luring Alligator to the base of a nearby mountain, where they had set a booby trap. When Alligator arrived at the scene the mountain fell on him and killed him. Following that, they fed Two-his-leg a gigantic roast with a large piece of earth inside it. When Two-his-leg had eaten his fill, he was too heavy to walk, and the twins took advantage of his condition by burying him alive. The twins had successfully disposed of not only Seven Macaw, but his sons as well.

Another Challenge

The Hero Twins soon took a new and even more challenging task. The boys were superb ballplayers, just like their father and their uncle; indeed, they frequently played pokatok on the same court where One Hunahpu and Seven Hunahpu had played when they were young. And just as their father and uncle had annoyed the lords of Xibalba with the constant bouncing of the ball on the court, so too did Hunahpu and Ixbalanque disturb the kings of the underworld as they played their games.

Remembering with satisfaction how they had killed One Hunahpu and Seven Hunahpu, the Lords of Death issued

the same challenge to the Hero Twins: Come to the under-world and play pokatok against the Lords of Xibalba. Like their father and uncle before them, Hunahpu and Ixbalanque eagerly accepted the invitation. But where One Hunahpu and Seven Hunahpu had no idea what lay ahead of them, the Hero Twins were much better prepared. They had been told by the gods about their relatives' journey—and had been given a detailed description of the tricks the Lords of Death had played. When they reached the rivers of pus and blood,

The Hero Twins prepare to play pokatok against the Lords of Xibalba.

The Twins and Their Grandmother

The Hero Twins' grandmother, Ixmukane, remembered very well that her own children, One Hunahpu and Seven Hunahpu, had been killed after traveling to Xibalba to play pokatok against the Lords of Death. She worried that if her grandchildren spent their time playing ball, they might suffer the same fate. According to the Popol Vuh, this concern impelled her to hide the ballplaying equipment that One Hunahpu and Seven Hunahpu had left in her house. Ixmukane hoped that the Hero Twins would never find the equipment and therefore would never be tempted to become ballplayers themselves.

The secret did not remain a secret forever, however. At one point, the story explains, Hunahpu and Ixbalanque were victimized by a practical joke played by a number of animals. Furious, they chased after the animals, but could catch only one—the mouse. They squeezed the mouse's throat, planning to choke it to death, but the mouse begged for its life. It assured the brothers that it knew an important secret and could help them regain property that was rightfully theirs. Curious, the brothers agreed to spare the mouse's life, whereupon it told them where Ixmukane had hidden the equipment.

The brothers smuggled the mouse inside the house, then used a pretext to send Ixmukane on an errand. While she was gone the mouse climbed to the hiding place and chewed through the ropes that tied the equipment together. According to this legend, that was the beginning of the twins' ballplaying career.

for instance, they were not alarmed; they were ready for the disgusting sight and floated calmly across each river without coming to harm.

Similarly, the Hero Twins knew that the lords had made puppets to fool their father and uncle. Determined not to fall into the same trap, the twins instructed a mosquito to bite each of the lords in turn. The first lords the mosquito bit failed to react; that told the twins that these were merely puppets. But when the mosquito started biting the figures in the shadows behind the puppets, each figure cried out in pain. Better yet, the lords called each other by name as they tried to figure out what was happening. "Just after Pus Master was bitten," Schuman writes, "Blood Gatherer responded, 'What is it, Pus Master?'"[69] In this way, Hunahpu and Ixbalanque quickly learned each lord's name.

When the boys arrived in the room where the puppets were set up, they avoided greeting the puppets. Instead, they went up to each lord in turn and called him by his name. The lords were impressed, but disappointed that the twins had not been fooled. Next, the lords offered the twins a seat on the red-hot rock that had burned One Hunahpu and Seven Hunahpu. Once again, though, the boys were too wise to be taken in. They recognized the seat for what it was and refused the offer. As the Popol Vuh notes approvingly, "They [the twins] were not to be fooled as were their fathers."[70]

For the next test, the lords sent the boys to the Dark House. Like their father and uncle, the boys were given torches and cigars and told to keep them alight all night long without burning them up. Though they knew that their father and uncle had been killed when they failed this test, Hunahpu and Ixbalanque kept calm. They placed a firefly at the end of each cigar and a reflective macaw feather at the end of each torch. From a distance, it appeared that the torches and cigars were burning. But in the morning the Lords of Death were dismayed to see that the torches and cigars were no smaller than they had been the previous evening. Once again the Hero Twins had outwitted their enemies.

Over the next few days the Lords of Xibalba gave the twins progressively more difficult tests. They locked the twins in a house filled with ice, but the brothers set fire to logs to keep from freezing. They imprisoned the twins in Jaguar House, described as "the jaguar-packed home of jaguars"[71] in one retelling of the story, but though the jaguars were starving the boys produced bones for the cats and survived. Even when Camazotz, the vampire bat, sliced off Hunahpu's head, Ixbalanque was able to find it and reattach it to his brother's body. The twins even won the promised game of pokatok against the lords.

Sacrifice and Victory

At this point, however, two prophets came to speak to the twins. They explained that in order to defeat the lords once and for all, the brothers would first have to allow themselves to be killed. When the lords built a bonfire and challenged

The Hero Twins engage in a final battle against the Lords of Death, from which they emerged victorious.

the boys to jump over it, the brothers accordingly jumped directly into the blazing fire. They burned to death, of course, but that was not enough for the lords. To make sure the twins would never return, the lords assembled the brothers' bones from the corpses, ground them into fine meal, and poured the meal into a river.

The lords were convinced they had gotten rid of the Hero Twins for good. They were wrong. As the prophets had foreseen, the bone meal rose to the surface of the river and formed itself back into the bodies of Hunahpu and Ixbalanque. The twins, fully alive once again, now disguised themselves as beggars who danced and performed miracles. Their most impressive trick, perhaps not surprisingly, was dying and coming back to life. "They would sacrifice themselves," Tedlock writes. "First they would kill themselves, but then they would suddenly look alive again."[72]

Word of the magical beggars soon reached the Lords of Death. Intrigued, the lords summoned the twins to their palace for a private performance. The lords began by demanding that the brothers sacrifice a dog and bring it back to life. The vagabonds did so. "The dog was truly happy when they revived him," notes the Popol Vuh. "He vigorously wagged his tail when they brought him back to life."[73] Next the brothers were told to set a house on fire and extinguish the blaze by magic. This they did as well. After that, they sacrificed a bystander and resurrected him, to the cheers of the lords. Finally, again at the urging of the lords, Ixbalanque killed Hunahpu, who quickly returned to life.

By now the lords of Xibalba were completely absorbed in the performance. Caught up in the excitement, two of them cried out to the beggars, "Do it to us! Sacrifice us!"[74] This was the moment the brothers had been waiting for. They promptly put both of the lords to death. They did not, however, bring their victims back to life. Instead, to the surprise and alarm of the lords, the twins identified themselves. It was immediately clear to the remaining lords that the brothers had powers that even the lords could not match. Terrified that they were about to die, the lords begged for mercy.

Hunahpu and Ixbalanque considered killing them all, but in the end they decided to offer the lords a deal. They agreed to restore the two dead lords to life and to refrain from killing the survivors. In exchange, the lords would have to agree to a sharp limitation of their powers. "Your day and your descendants will not be great," the twins told the lords, promising that the lords would henceforth be called "masters of stupidity."[75] Moreover, the twins demanded that the lords lead them to the place where One Hunahpu and Seven Hunahpu had been buried. They brought their relatives back to life, then left the earth for good. According to one tradition, Hunahpu ascended to the sky and became the sun, while Ixbalanque became the moon.

Hero Twins in Stone

In 2009 archaeologists found two enormous stone carvings depicting the Hero Twins at a Mayan site in present-day Guatemala. Each stone is about 26 feet (8m) tall.

Intelligence, Sacrifice, and Power

The tale of the Hero Twins includes a number of elements that help illustrate the lives and values of the Mayan people. For one, though Hunahpu and Ixbalanque occasionally used their strength or their magical powers to defeat their enemies, they more frequently used their brains to win against their foes. They tricked two of the Lords of Death into sacrificing themselves, for example, and they fooled their enemies into believing that the torches and cigars were lit all night long. This emphasis on cleverness was not accidental. Among the Maya, brute force was not valued nearly as much as intelligence and creativity. As Linda Schele and David Freidel write, "The Hero of the Maya did not overpower his enemies: He outwitted them."[76]

A second theme involves sacrifice. The Maya are far from the only culture to tell stories about self-sacrifice leading to a greater victory; a similar story appears, for example, in the Christian narrative, which describes how Jesus allows himself to be put to death, only to be brought back to life shortly afterwards. The Hero Twins saga demonstrates the Mayan belief, shared with Christianity and other traditions, that even the very worst of events can sometimes have a positive outcome. Indeed, the Mayan legend suggests that only by submitting to death can death be overcome. This idea is connected to a number of Mayan traditions, notably the custom of bloodletting: Through the pain of ritual cutting and piercing, the Maya believed they were improving their odds of reaching heaven after death.

Some writers have pointed out, in particular, that the sacrificial aspects of the story relate to the cycle of planting and harvesting maize. Each successive maize crop must die to provide food so that the people might live. This, in itself, is a form of sacrifice on the part of the corn. In addition, the harvesting of one crop is followed shortly by the planting of another. The second planting, in

An Evil Place

In her science fiction novel *A Wrinkle in Time,* published in 1962, author Madeleine L'Engle named a mythical planet Camazotz, after the vampire bat that sliced off the head of one of the Hero Twins. Not surprisingly, Camazotz the planet is a frightening place overrun by evil.

this way, represents a rebirth of sorts. And the planting of the maize seeds also connects to the theme of sacrifice and death. By burying the seed in order to get it to germinate and grow, Coe theorizes, "the Maya farmer symbolically sent [the seed] to Xibalba, to its temporary death."[77]

The story of Seven Macaw, too, indicates the values of the Maya. Seven Macaw was certainly beautiful, but only on the outside; he was arrogant rather than humble and selfish rather than kind. His downfall represents the danger of having rulers who are only concerned with outward appearance and personal glorification. Indeed, Mayan kings often wore macaw feathers in their headdresses to remind them of the fate of Seven Macaw—and to prompt them to exercise their power wisely. "Properly used," write Schele, Freidel, and Joy

A fresco depicts several royal Mayan figures, including a king wearing macaw feathers on his head as a symbol of humility and kindness.

Parker, "this power preserved cosmos and country. Improperly used, like [Seven Macaw's] arrogance, it became empty strength and a danger to all around."[78]

Filled with interesting characters, dramatic events, and cleverness on the part of the heroes, the saga of the Hero Twins is in many ways distinctly Mayan. The importance of pokatok in the myth, for example, marks the tale as Central American. Similarly, the mentions of subtropical animals such as macaws and jaguars also suggest the story's geographic origins. Nonetheless, the story's themes are universal. The tale of the Hero Twins touches on questions and issues familiar to people all over the world: revenge and deception, arrogance and humility, bloodshed and sacrifice, beauty and power. In particular, the story illustrates the struggle between good and evil and offers hope that humanity can eventually triumph over death. The tale of the Hero Twins represents one of the finest works of mythology in any culture.

CHAPTER 5

Mythology, the Maya, and the World

The two best-known stories in Mayan mythology are undoubtedly the creation legend and the saga of the Hero Twins. But the Mayan tradition includes a wide variety of myths and legends beyond these two. Like the stories about the Hero Twins and the creation of the world, these lesser-known myths are uniquely Mayan. It is clear that they sprang from the experiences, values, and beliefs of a particular culture living in a particular part of the world. At the same time, though, many of the themes in Mayan mythology are universal, and there are strong parallels between the myths and legends of the Maya and the myths and legends from other cultures. The myths of the Maya speak not just to the concerns and values of the Maya themselves. On the contrary, they reflect issues that are common the world over.

The Chirimia

One excellent example of the universal nature of Mayan myths is a legend often known as the story of the chirimia. The myth tells of a chatty, cheerful young princess who suddenly sinks into a deep depression. To her father's alarm, she stops speaking and smiling. The king does his best to lighten her mood. As author Jane Anne Volkmer writes in her retelling of the story, "He gave her glistening jade birds from the highlands. He had his hunters bring exotic birds to her from the jungle. He called the best ballplayers in the kingdom to play in the ballcourt before her."[79] But the princess's depression only worsens.

Searching for a solution, one of the king's advisers points out that the princess is now of marriageable age. Accordingly, the king summons the wealthiest and handsomest bachelors of his kingdom to court his daughter. They woo

Mayan musicians play a drum and a chirimia, a wind instrument that, according to myth, was first created out of a tree branch by the god of the forest to please a princess.

her with expensive gifts and high-flown speeches, but the princess shows no interest. Later that day, however, after all the suitors have gone home, the princess hears a young man singing outside the palace. Though he has no rank and no wealth, his voice is sweet and pleasing. The young woman listens, and for the first time in days, she smiles.

Ignoring the young man's lack of social and economic standing—not to mention the fact that no one knows who this man is or where he is from—the king quickly offers the stranger his daughter's hand in marriage. The princess is attracted to the man; however, she is not ready to make a commitment to him. As much as she appreciates his voice, she tells him, she does not like it as much as she enjoys the singing of birds. Nonetheless, she offers the young man an opportunity to win her. "If you can make your song and your voice become one as the birds do," she tells him, "I shall marry you."[80]

The young man is eager to try. He heads into the woods, where he spends two months listening to the birds and imitating their singing style. His efforts, though, are to no avail. He is ready to give up, when he receives an unexpected visit from the god of the forest. The god transforms a tree branch into a hollow pipe with holes and tells the young man that this is a musical instrument called a chirimia. "He instructed the young man exactly how to blow into one end while moving his fingers over the holes," reads one version of the myth. "The notes of the birds tumbled out, clear and sweet."[81] Returning to the palace, the man plays his instrument outside the princess's window. The princess's depression ends, and the story concludes with a wedding.

Pik and Chac Play Pokatok

Mayan mythology has inspired some modern authors to write original stories that use Mayan gods and goddesses and themes. For example, David Wisniewski's story *Rain Player* tells of a boy named Pik who challenges Chac, the god of rain, to a game of pokatok during a time of drought.

Themes and Images

The tale of the chirimia is easy to identify as Mayan. The story includes a reference to the Mayan sport of pokatok, for example. The princess receives gifts that are highly prized in Mayan culture, such as jade, quetzal feathers, and cacao beans, which are used to make chocolate. And some versions echo the Mayan emphasis on time by detailing just when in the king's reign each of the events of the story took place. Volkmer's retelling, for example, notes that the princess was born "on the night of the 20th full moon"[82] of her father's rule—that is, about twenty months after he took office.

At the same time, though, the story of the chirimia is reminiscent of other myths, legends, and fairy tales from across the globe. Indeed, it has many elements that should be familiar to anyone who has read folk stories from other cultures. For example, this myth downplays the importance of nobility and wealth: Though rich and important suitors fail to capture the heart of the princess, a young man with no social position succeeds. This message is reminiscent of the European fairy tale of Cinderella, in which the prince marries a servant girl who sits among the ashes rather than any of the high-born, elegant ladies he could have chosen.

The chirimia story includes other common themes as well; for instance, that of being assigned a task that at first seems impossible. Many traditional myths and stories use this theme. Ancient Greek myths about a figure named Heracles, or Hercules, are a good example. In one of these myths, Hercules is assigned a series of complicated labors: cleaning an enormous stable, stealing valuable items from gods, defeating monsters in combat. Though many of the tasks appear to be too much for any one man to accomplish, Hercules eventually completes them all. Just as the young man in the chirimia story does the impossible by making music as beautifully as the birds, so too does Hercules accomplish tasks that most people would argue could never be done.

A third important motif in the chirimia story is that the young man receives assistance from the forest god. The theme of help from supernatural beings also crosses cultural boundaries in mythology and folklore. In the story of Cinderella, for example, a fairy godmother uses magic to allow Cinderella to attend the dance at the castle where she meets her prince. A Korean legend called "The Fox Sister" has a similar theme. In this myth, three men are being chased by a fox spirit that hopes to kill them. A mysterious man gives the

Sources

The classical period of Mayan culture ended more than a thousand years ago. Many of the original writings that date from this era are no longer in existence. Some were written on impermanent paper made from bark and have disintegrated in the humid rain forest. Others were deliberately destroyed by the Spanish conquerors. Only a few books and inscriptions survive from this period. Thus, much of what is known today about Mayan mythology comes from the oral tradition—that is, from legends passed down from one generation to the next through storytelling.

A few of these legends, including the myths in the Popol Vuh, were committed to paper after the arrival of the Spanish. Others, however, were not recorded until the twentieth century. Given the political, religious, and linguistic changes in Central America since the heyday of the Maya, it is not surprising that many of these stories seem more European than Mayan. Quite a few reflect cultural and religious traditions brought by the Spanish five centuries ago. Even the titles of now-traditional Mayan stories such as "How the Christ Child Was Warmed" reflect the impact of European ideas and images.

Remarkably, however, despite the long passage of time since the classical era, and despite the significant changes in Central American history since the 1500s, many other legends still told in the modern era have changed very little over time. That is particularly true of the Lacandon, a Mayan group living primarily in the Mexican state of Chiapas. "Many of their stories show no European influence whatsoever," writes folklorist John Bierhorst. There is a good chance, then, that at least some of the tales popular among the present-day Lacandon were told in essentially the same form more than a millennium ago by their ancestors.

John Bierhorst, ed. *The Monkey's Haircut*. New York: Morrow, 1986, p. 6.

brothers three magical bottles and instructs them to throw the bottles over their shoulder when the spirit approaches. The bottles smash on the ground and turn into a thicket, a river, and a fire, which slow the spirit and allow the brothers to escape.

Myths, Gods, and People

Interactions between humans and gods, in fact, are common throughout the Mayan tradition. An excellent example appears in a story about the rain god, Chac. In this myth,

Chac travels to earth to look for a servant. Finding a boy who seems like a good candidate, Chac brings him up into the sky. However, the boy constantly causes trouble. At one point, he chops down a tree after having been specifically told not to. The tree falls directly on him, and Chac has to come and pry it off his body. Later, the boy commands Chac's griddle to produce a constant stream of tortillas. The griddle cooks tortilla after tortilla until the boy is buried beneath them. Again, Chac comes to the rescue.

Matters finally come to a head one night. As the story explains, Chac has a set of tools that he uses to bring weather to the earth. Two of these tools are particularly important. One is a large bag that contains the winds. When Chac chooses to make the winds blow on earth, he simply opens the bag; the wider the bag is opened, the stronger the wind blows. The other tool is a gourd filled with water. To bring rain, Chac sprinkles some of this water over the earth. Not

A statute depicts Chac, the Mayan god of rain, one of many deities that mythology depicts as interacting with humans.

surprisingly, Chac's disobedient servant wants to try out these tools and see what it is like to be a god. Equally unsurprisingly, given the boy's track record, Chac flatly refuses to allow the boy to so much as touch the equipment.

The boy, however, ignores the order. After Chac falls asleep, the young servant sneaks into the rain god's quarters and runs off with the bag and the gourd. First, he rips open the bag, and all the winds escape. "The winds went screeching off," writes folklorist John Bierhorst in his version of the myth, "and a terrific storm rushed down on the world."[83] The boy is not strong enough to close the bag, and the winds continue to blow ferociously. Similarly, the boy pours all the water out of the gourd instead of sprinkling it lightly, an action that causes torrential rains. At that point the winds seize the boy, send him plummeting toward the earth, and break him into pieces.

Chac sleeps through the beginning of this minidrama. When morning arrives and he wakes up, though, he quickly deduces what has happened. Borrowing new equipment from another of the rain gods, Chac corrals the winds and stops the storm. Then he finds the boy and brings him back to life. By this time, however, Chac has had enough. "I don't want you for my servant," Chac says. "You disobey and steal! Go back where you came from!"[84] The boy is glad to do so. Returning to his house, he proudly tells his brother—who of course has just survived the most damaging storm imaginable—that he was the cause of the disaster. "Wasn't it fun?"[85] he asks, irrepressible—and oblivious—to the end.

Parallels

The myth of the chirimia and the legend of Chac and his servant are far from the only Mayan myths to depict interaction between people and the gods. In a story sometimes called "Lord Sun's Bride," for instance, the sun god courts and eventually marries a mortal. And a story from the Popol Vuh describes how the leaders of the early Mayan people sent two beautiful young women to swim in a creek in hopes of seducing three of the gods. In the world of Mayan mythology, in fact, it is perfectly normal for gods and humans to cross paths. Though they do not inhabit the same part of

Historical Fiction in Film

The 2006 movie *Apocalypto*, directed by Mel Gibson, is set in Mayan territory toward the end of the classical era. Though the plot is fictional, the film includes some accurate information about Mayan society and religion.

the world—in Mayan tradition, gods and goddesses usually live in the sky or in Xibalba, while humans make their homes on the earth—they nonetheless interact regularly.

By showing connections between the gods and the people, Mayan myths do not seek to put mortals and deities on the same plane. In the myth of Chac and his servant, Chac is clearly much more powerful than the boy. Chac can fly; Chac can control the bag of winds; Chac can restore the servant to life; the boy can do none of these things. Likewise, in the story of the chirimia, the young man must learn from the god, not the other way around. At the same time, though, showing communication between the gods and the mortals is a way of expressing the Mayan worldview. The Maya believed that the gods were present at all times in the lives of ordinary people, and these myths emphasize that perspective. The gods, in short, are so much a part of everyday activity that it does not seem unusual for Chac to speak directly to a Mayan child.

Myths like these also present the gods as accessible to human beings. Instead of describing Chac as a disembodied force somewhere off in the distant skies, the story of Chac and his servant helps to bring Chac to life. It shows him having thoughts and feelings much like the thoughts and feelings of human beings. "Lord Sun's Bride" is similar. At one point in the narrative, for instance, the sun god stuffs a deerskin with ashes and sets it on his shoulder. He hopes that the young woman he admires will think he is a mighty hunter. However, he slips, the deerskin splits, and his trickery is revealed. "Lord Sun ran off," one version of the story reports. "He was ashamed."[86] In this moment Lord Sun is not at all a distant, all-powerful deity; his reaction, in fact, is much the same as any ordinary person's might be.

These connections between humans and gods also arise in the myths, legends, and religious narratives of many other cultures. For instance, a story from Cameroon in Africa tells of a young woman named Beebyeebyee who meets a water god while she is fishing. The god immediately asks her to marry him, and she agrees. "He was extremely handsome," one version of the myth explains, "so Beebyeebyee and the water god got married then and there."[87] Another legend, this one from Greece, tells how the goddess Athena took part in a weaving contest against an ordinary mortal named Arachne. Though Arachne wove a beautiful design, she lost the contest when Athena's finished product had what one reteller describes as "a perfection that only a goddess could achieve."[88]

Likewise, myths and legends from a variety of places also personify deities the way Mayan mythology does. Legends about the Roman goddess Juno, for example, describe her as easily angered when her husband, Jupiter, romances other women. Similarly, one legend about the Babylonian demigod Gilgamesh shows him deeply distressed over the death of a friend. And in Norse mythology, the god Loki often becomes envious of other gods or of mortals. In some cases Loki even kills others out of spite or anger when his jealousy gets the best of him. The desire to make the gods seem more real and more human, then, is not a desire specific to the Maya. Rather, it is a trait common among many cultures all around the globe.

Fire and Sacrifice

While some Mayan myths describe the adventures of gods and mortals, others serve to explain why the world is the way it is. One example, sometimes called "The Gift of Fire," is set during a very early period in Mayan mythology. Indeed, the story takes place shortly after the various tribes developed from the original four founding families. According to the legend, the tribes all traveled together to a place known as Seven Caves, Seven Canyons. Whatever the virtues of this spot, a tropical climate was not among them. At night, the temperature in Seven Caves, Seven Canyons dropped substantially. The people of the tribes had no warm clothing and no knowledge of fire. As a result, they nearly froze to death each night.

One evening, however, a Mayan god named Tojil set a fire ablaze in the wilderness. Two of the founding fathers,

A terra-cotta sculpture shows the face of the Mayan god of fire. Mayan mythology includes a story of how fire was first presented to man.

Jaguar Quitze and Jaguar Night, saw the fire. Though they did not know exactly what it was, they quickly realized that its heat could keep them warm. They begged Tojil to give them some of his fire. In exchange, they promised that they, their families, and their descendants would always think of Tojil as their own special god, a god that they would single out for particular praise. Tojil was happy to accept, and he readily gave some of his fire to the tribes headed by Jaguar Quitze and Jaguar Night. "I am your god: so be it," Tojil told them. "I am your lord: so be it."[89]

The members of the other Mayan tribes, however, were still as cold as ever. Desperate for relief, they approached the tribes that were warming themselves by the new fire. "Have pity on us," they begged. "Give us some of your fire. We are dying from the cold."[90] At that moment, however, a man with the wings of a bat appeared to Jaguar Quitze and Jaguar Night. The newcomer was an emissary from the gods, and he told Jaguar Quitze and Jaguar Night that they should not simply share their fire with the others. Fire, he reminded them, was a gift from the god Tojil. If the tribes without fire wanted to warm up, the messenger explained, they would have to make an offering to Tojil. Not just any offering would do, however. The gods had a specific offering in mind: human sacrifice. At some point in the future, the emissary explained, Tojil would demand that the members of these tribes and their descendants sacrifice themselves or each other. Whenever Tojil decided to seek proof of their loyalty, Dennis Tedlock writes, "all the tribes [would] be cut open before him, and . . . their hearts [would] be removed through their sides, under their arms."[91] Despite the certainty that they would someday have to follow through with these sacrifices, the tribes agreed without hesitation. They received the fire as promised, making the nights at Seven Caves, Seven Canyons much more bearable.

Connections

"The Gift of Fire" explains several important aspects of Mayan history, religion, and culture. Most obviously, of course, it describes how the Maya obtained and learned to use fire. But the legend also emphasizes that the relationships between the gods and their people are based on a contract of sorts: The tribes agree to single out Tojil for particular praise if Tojil will give them the fire they need. Moreover, the story shows the importance of human sacrifice as a symbol of the loyalty that the Maya felt to their gods. In each case, "The Gift of Fire" offers a window into how the Maya viewed their world and the connection they perceived to the deities who ruled it.

Themes and images such as the ones found in "The Gift of Fire" also appear in stories from traditions across the world. The bringing of fire to the

Mayan Myths in Modern Literature

Mayan myths are referenced in some comic books and children's and young adult literature. Examples include Walt Disney's *Uncle Scrooge Adventures: Crown of the Maya*; Jerry West's *The Happy Hollisters and the Mystery of the Mexican Idol*; and the *Joshua Files* series by M.G. Harris.

people is a particularly common topic. In Greek mythology, for instance, a famous legend tells how a god named Prometheus stole fire from the ruler of the gods, Zeus, and gave it to the people of Greece. A similar North American myth credits the raven with showing human beings how to build and control fire. And legends from elsewhere in modern-day Mexico describe how the lowly opossum dipped its tail into a fire and carried the flame back to the people. "I, Opossum, promise to give you fire," he told the people, "if you promise never to eat me."[92] The people accepted the deal, and so fire came into the human world for the first time.

An ancient mosaic depicts Prometheus presenting fire to the Greeks in a story that is similar to the fire myth found in other ancient traditions, including that of the Maya.

Likewise, the contractual ties between people and gods are expressed in a variety of traditions. The notion that gods and people are bound to one another is especially prevalent, for example, in Judaism and Christianity. The book of Jeremiah in the Hebrew Bible shows God making a series of promises to the people of Israel. In exchange for giving them special treatment, he tells them, they must agree that they will worship no other god but him. "You will be my people," he explains, "and I will be your God" (Jer. 30:22). "The Gift of Fire" has obvious parallels with this story.

Animals

Where "The Gift of Fire" explains events in the lives of humans, other Mayan myths focus more on animals. One example is a story called "How the Peacock Got Its Feathers." In this myth, the peacock and its mate, the peahen, began as gray birds with unremarkable plumage. The peahen, however, had always yearned for brightly colored feathers. Unable to grow them herself, she decided to steal Chac's headdress, which—in one writer's description—was made up of "long, shining feathers woven of gold, silk, and rainbows."[93] Eager to become beautiful, the peahen went to Chac's house, waited until he fell asleep, and then flew off with the feathers in her beak.

The peahen decided to wear most of the feathers over her tail, placing only a handful on top of her head. The other birds were much amazed when the peahen appeared in front of them. Though they did not recognize her, they were struck by her beauty. Her husband, the peacock, however, knew exactly who she was, and he was furious when he realized that she had stolen the feathers. Quickly, he flew off to find Chac. "Your headdress has been stolen by my mate," he told the rain god, "and she is wearing the feathers on her rear end!"[94]

Together, Chac and the peacock hurried to the assembled birds. Stripping the peahen of the headdress, Chac revealed that the beautiful new bird was neither beautiful nor new—only the ordinary, drab peahen they had all

Disobedience

The theme of disobedience is a common one in Mayan myths. One example is the story of Chac and his servant. Again and again, the boy does what he pleases and ignores the instructions that Chac gives him. Unfortunately for the boy, there are unpleasant consequences for his disobedience. No one wants to be struck by a falling tree, or to be buried beneath a steady stream of tortillas, no matter how tasty they may be. And when the boy's defiance causes the storm, in particular, the penalty is enormous: The people experience one of the worst and most destructive storms imaginable, and the boy himself is killed. Only the intervention of Chac stops the storm and brings the boy back to life. In some sense, then, this legend is a cautionary tale about what happens when people disobey the gods.

Other cultures, too, often include themes of disobedience—and the consequences of disobedience—in their myths, legends, and stories. In the Greek myth of Orpheus and Eurydice, for instance, Orpheus is allowed to bring his beloved wife, Eurydice, back from the underworld. He is told that she will follow him on the path from the underworld up to the surface of the earth. He is also told, however, that he must not look back at her until both are safely on the earth once more. When he disobeys this instruction, the gods whisk her back to the underworld, and Orpheus never sees her again. Similar themes of disobedience appear in the legends and tales of societies as diverse as the early Chinese, the aboriginal peoples of Australia, and the Hebrews of the Middle East.

Orpheus loses his wife Eurydice to the underworld after disobeying an order not to look at her.

known for years. Chac then presented the headdress to the peacock and helped him stretch the feathers like a fan over his own tail. Because the peacock had prevented the peahen from getting away with her crime, Chac told the rest of the birds, he deserved to wear the feathers. From then on, the myth concludes, every peacock has had a shiny fan of tailfeathers, matching Chac's original headdress, but every peahen is plain.

Toads, Opossums, and Bluebirds

Another example from the Mayan tradition describes how toads got their wide stomachs. In this story, Toad hitches a ride into the sky with his friend Hawk. Once in the sky, however, Hawk leaves Toad on a cloud and flies away. Realizing he has no other way to get back down to the ground, Toad decides to jump. He hopes to glide gently toward the earth, just as Hawk is able to do. But instead of soaring majestically through the sky, Toad plummets like a rock. "When he hit the earth," one account explains, "he flattened out. He landed hard, and his belly spread out wide. That's why the toad today has a big belly."[95]

As with other types of stories, myths explaining why animals look and act the way they do are also widespread in different traditions. One example is the Mexican tale of how the opossum brought fire to the people. By using his tail to carry the fire, the legend explains, the opossum burned all the fur off his tail, leaving it completely hairless. Another legend, this one told among the Pima Indians of the American Southwest, explains that the bluebird is blue because he bathed in the blue water of a lake. "There lies the place, the blue water place," the bluebird remarks after realizing that he has changed color. "I bathed in that water. Now I am blue too!"[96]

The fullness of Mayan mythology is readily apparent in stories such as the legend of the chirimia, the tale of Chac and his servant, and the account of how the peacock got its feathers. These myths and legends cover a great range as well; they are about a variety of topics and appear in a variety of styles. Some of these stories are intended to be

A Mayan mural includes a figure of a toad, which, according to myth, developed its wide belly after plummeting to the earth from a cloud.

funny and light, while others are much more serious. Some have happy endings, others do not. Some are told from the perspective of the gods, while others adopt the viewpoint of ordinary humans.

Like the Mayan creation saga and the narrative of the Hero Twins, these stories shape and reflect the rich culture of the Mayan people. But as the parallels between the myths of the Maya and the legends and narratives of other peoples make clear, the concerns of Mayan mythology are not simply Mayan. Rather, they discuss themes that are worldwide— themes that touch us all.

NOTES

Introduction: Rise and Fall

1. Ake Hultkrantz. *The Religions of the American Indians*. Berkeley: University of California, 1979, p. 206.
2. Michael D. Coe. *The Maya*. New York: Thames and Hudson, 2011, p. 169.

Chapter 1: The Maya

3. Linda Schele and David Freidel. *A Forest of Kings: The Untold Story of the Ancient Maya*. New York: Morrow, 1990, p. 66.
4. Victor Montejo. *Popol Vuh*. Toronto: Groundwood, 1999, p. 33.
5. John S. Henderson. *The World of the Ancient Maya*. Ithaca, NY: Cornell University Press, 1981, p. 85.
6. Quoted in J. Eric S. Thompson. *Maya History and Religion*. Norman: University of Oklahoma Press, 1970, p. 191.
7. Quoted in Thompson. *Maya History and Religion*, p. 189.
8. Coe, *The Maya*, p. 230.
9. David Carrasco. *Religions of Mesoamerica*. Prospect Heights, IL: Waveland Press, 1990, p. 110.
10. Coe. *The Maya*, p. 229.
11. Quoted in Henderson. *The World of the Ancient Maya*, pp. 212–213.
12. Schele and Freidel. *A Forest of Kings*, p. 66.
13. Carrasco. *Religions of Mesoamerica*, p. 94.
14. Carrasco. *Religions of Mesoamerica*, p. 105.
15. The Metropolitan Museum of Art. "Special Exhibitions: Treasures of Ancient Maya Kings," 2006. www.metmuseum.org/exhibitions/listings/2006/maya%20treasures.
16. Carrasco. *Religions of Mesoamerica*, pp. 103–104.
17. Mary Ellen Miller. *Maya Art and Architecture*. New York: Thames and Hudson, 1999, p. 11.
18. Coe. *The Maya*, p. 121.
19. Henderson. *The World of the Ancient Maya*, p. 45.
20. Quoted in Coe. *The Maya*, p. 18.

Chapter 2: Gods and Goddesses

21. Coe. *The Maya*, p. 223.
22. Leonard Everett Fisher. *Gods and Goddesses of the Ancient Maya*. New York: Holiday House, 1999, p. 9.
23. Henderson. *The World of the Ancient Maya*, p. 85.
24. Fisher. *Gods and Goddesses of the Ancient Maya*, p. 9.

25. Thompson. *Maya History and Religion*, p. 233.
26. Quoted in Miller. *Maya Art and Architecture*, p. 61.
27. Thompson. *Maya History and Religion*, p. 211.
28. Quoted in Thompson. *Maya History and Religion*, p. 312.
29. Quoted in Marta Weigle. *Spiders and Spinsters: Women and Mythology*. Santa Fe: Sunstone, 2007, p. 167.
30. Coe. *The Maya*, p. 224.
31. Fisher. *Gods and Goddesses of the Ancient Maya*, p. 11.
32. M.E. Kampen. *The Religion of the Maya*. Leyden, The Netherlands: E.J. Brill, 1981, p. 25.
33. Robert J. Sharer and Sylvanus Griswold Morley. *The Ancient Maya*. Stanford, CA: Stanford University Press, 1993, p. 532.
34. Fisher. *Gods and Goddesses of the Ancient Maya*, p. 13.
35. C. Scott Littleton. *Gods, Goddesses, and Mythology*. Vol. 6. Tarrytown, NY: Marshall Cavendish, 2005, p. 847.
36. Anne Rockwell. *The Boy Who Wouldn't Obey*. New York: Greenwillow, 2000.
37. Henderson. *The World of the Ancient Maya*, p. 85.
38. Miller. *Maya Art and Architecture*, p. 162.
39. Fisher. *Gods and Goddesses of the Ancient Maya*, p. 27.
40. Sharer and Morley. *The Ancient Maya*, p. 535.
41. Lewis Spence. *Magic and Mysteries of Mexico*. London: Rider, n.d., p. 124.
42. Fisher. *Gods and Goddesses of the Ancient Maya*, p. 29.

Chapter 3: Creation

43. David Adams Leeming. *Creation Myths of the World*. Santa Barbara, CA: ABC-CLIO, 2010, p. xx.
44. Quoted in Schele and Freidel. *A Forest of Kings*, p. 246.
45. Schele and Freidel. *A Forest of Kings*, p. 252.
46. Quoted in Richard A. Wertime and Angela M.H. Schuster, "Written in the Stars." In *Secrets of the Maya* by Archaeology, Inc. New York: Hatherleigh, 2003, p. 81.
47. Montejo. *Popol Vuh*, p. 13.
48. Dennis Tedlock. *Popol Vuh: The Mayan Book of the Dawn of Life*. New York: Simon and Schuster, 1985, p. 72.
49. Quoted in Carrasco. *Religions of Mesoamerica*, p. 99.
50. Montejo. *Popol Vuh*, p. 14.
51. Quoted in Gene S. Stuart and George E. Stuart. *Lost Kingdoms of the Maya*. Washington, DC: National Geographic, 1993, p, 46.
52. Montejo. *Popol Vuh*, p. 15.
53. Quoted in Schele and Freidel. *A Forest of Kings*, p. 476.
54. Deborah Nourse Lattimore. *Why There Is No Arguing in Heaven*. New York: Harper and Row, 1989.
55. Tedlock. *Popol Vuh*, p. 83.

56. Michael A. Schuman. *Mayan and Aztec Mythology.* Berkeley Heights, NJ: Enslow, 2001, p. 26.
57. Tedlock. *Popol Vuh*, p. 84.
58. Montejo. *Popol Vuh*, p. 19.
59. Allen J. Christenson. *Popol Vuh: The Sacred Book of the Maya.* New York: O Books, 2003, p. 197.
60. Montejo. *Popol Vuh*, p. 63.
61. Montejo. *Popol Vuh*, p. 64.

Chapter 4: The Hero Twins

62. Tedlock. *Popol Vuh*, p. 105.
63. Christenson. *Popol Vuh*, p. 115.
64. Tedlock. *Popol Vuh*, p. 111.
65. Tedlock. *Popol Vuh*, p. 111.
66. Tedlock. *Popol Vuh*, p. 117.
67. Coe. *The Maya*, p. 68.
68. Schuman. *Mayan and Aztec Mythology*, p. 39.
69. Schuman. *Mayan and Aztec Mythology*, p. 64.
70. Montejo. *Popol Vuh*, p. 50.
71. Quoted in Carrasco. *Religions of Mesoamerica*, p. 120.
72. Tedlock. *Popol Vuh*, p. 151.
73. Christenson. *Popol Vuh*, p. 183.
74. Quoted in Carrasco, *Religions of Mesoamerica*, p. 121.
75. Tedlock. *Popol Vuh*, p. 158.
76. Schele and Freidel, *A Forest of Kings*, p. 76.
77. Coe. *The Maya*, p. 68.
78. David Freidel, Linda Schele, and Joy Parker. *Maya Cosmos: Three Thousand Years on the Shaman's Path.* New York: Morrow, 1993, p. 211.

Chapter 5: Mythology, the Maya, and the World

79. Jane Anne Volkmer. *Song of the Chirimia.* Minneapolis: Carolrhoda, 1990.
80. Volkmer, *Song of the Chirimia.*
81. Quoted in Malena Kuss. *Music in Latin America and the Caribbean.* Austin: University of Texas Press, 2004, p. 319.
82. Volkmer. *Song of the Chirimia.*
83. John Bierhorst, ed. *The Monkey's Haircut.* New York: Morrow, 1986, p. 68.
84. Rockwell. *The Boy Who Wouldn't Obey.*
85. Bierhorst, ed. *The Monkey's Haircut*, p. 69.
86. Bierhorst, ed. *The Monkey's Haircut*, p. 85.
87. Katrin Tchana. *The Serpent Slayer.* Boston: Little, Brown, 2000, p. 38.
88. Amy Turnbull, *Greek Myths.* Somerville, MA: Candlewick, 2011.
89. Tedlock. *Popol Vuh*, p. 172.
90. Montejo. *Popol Vuh,* p. 66.
91. Tedlock. *Popol Vuh*, pp. 174–175.
92. John Bierhorst. *The Mythology of Mexico and Central America.* New York: Morrow, 1990, p. 77.
93. Sandy Sepehri. *How the Peacock Got Its Feathers.* Vero Beach, FL: Rourke, 2007.
94. Sepehri. *How the Peacock Got Its Feathers.*
95. Bierhorst, ed. *The Monkey's Haircut*, p. 137.
96. Ari Berk and Carolyn Dunn. *Coyote Speaks.* New York: Abrams, 2008, p. 113.

archaeologist: A scientist who studies people of the distant past.

benevolence: Good will, kindness.

bloodletting: The cutting or piercing of the body to draw blood for religious reasons.

chirimia: A musical instrument similar to a flute or oboe.

city-state: A governmental unit consisting of a city and some surrounding rural areas that functions as an independent unit.

deity: A god or goddess.

drought: An extended period of lower-than-normal rainfall.

glyph: A symbol used in Mayan writing.

maize: Corn.

malevolence: Evil, wickedness.

milpa: A field used for farming by the Maya.

pokatok: A ball game popular in the ancient Mayan world.

Popol Vuh: A book containing some of the most important legends of the Maya.

sacrifice: To give something up, or make an offering to a deity; in some ancient cultures animals and people were killed as offerings to the gods.

scribe: A person who writes down the words of others.

Tikal: One of the largest and most important Mayan cities during the classical era and home of the tallest Mayan pyramid.

Wacah Chan: The "world tree" of Mayan mythology; the central point of the earth.

Xibalba: The underworld in Mayan mythology.

Books

Archaeology, Inc. *Secrets of the Maya.* New York: Hatherleigh, 2003. A collection of articles about Mayan sites that originally appeared in *Archaeology* magazine. Some of the articles include discoveries related to the Mayan myths and legends.

John Bierhorst, ed. *The Monkey's Haircut.* New York: Morrow, 1986. A valuable collection of Mayan folktales, some collected recently, others dating back centuries. Some of the tales, though not all, are myths and legends.

John Bierhorst. *The Mythology of Mexico and Central America.* New York: Morrow, 1990. An introduction to the traditional mythology of the Maya, the Aztec, and other peoples of Mesoamerica. Includes a few examples of myths told among these peoples as well.

Ann Bingham and Jeremy Roberts. *South and Meso-American Mythology A to Z.* New York: Chelsea House, 2010. This one-volume encyclopedia presents useful information on the myths and legends of the Maya, along with other peoples of Mexico and Latin America.

Allen J. Christenson. *Popol Vuh: The Sacred Book of the Maya.* New York: O Books, 2003. One of several retellings of the Popol Vuh available today, this translation is well written and thorough. The book also includes notes that help explain the images and events of the Popol Vuh in the context of the Mayan world.

Michael D. Coe. *The Maya.* New York: Thames and Hudson, 2011. A thorough investigation of Mayan culture and society. Though the emphasis is not specifically on religion or mythology, the book has some useful information on these subjects and places the mythology within the context of the Mayan world very well.

Leonard Everett Fisher. *Gods and Goddesses of the Ancient Maya.* New York: Holiday House, 1999. Short and simple, this volume includes detailed images of Mayan deities along with brief summaries of their characteristics and responsibilities.

Nathaniel Harris. *Ancient Maya.* Washington, DC: National Geographic, 2008. A short, well-illustrated volume that focuses on the discoveries of archaeologists at Mayan sites. Includes some information on gods, goddesses, and religious practices.

David Adams Leeming. *Creation Myths of the World.* Santa Barbara, CA: ABC-

CLIO, 2010. Summaries of various creation stories, including the one that appears in the Popol Vuh. Includes some background information about the cultures as well.

C. Scott Littleton. *Gods, Goddesses, and Mythology*. Tarrytown, NY: Marshall Cavendish, 2005. This multivolume encyclopedia is detailed and informative yet accessible. The set includes information about the mythologies of dozens of cultures; volume 6 includes the Maya.

Mary Ellen Miller. *Maya Art and Architecture*. New York: Thames and Hudson, 1999. An excellent overview of the Maya as artists and builders, which provides much information about Mayan religious beliefs and the connections between art and worship. Exceptionally well illustrated.

Victor Montejo. *Popol Vuh*. Toronto: Groundwood, 1999. Montejo is an author and anthropologist originally from Guatemala. This is a somewhat abridged but nevertheless accurate retelling of the Popol Vuh. Well written, easy to read, and nicely illustrated.

Michael A. Schuman. *Mayan and Aztec Mythology*. Berkeley Heights, NJ: Enslow, 2001. A short retelling of important myths from the Aztec and Mayan traditions. Includes excerpts from commentaries by people who have closely studied the legends of these peoples.

Dennis Tedlock. *Popol Vuh: The Mayan Book of the Dawn of Life*. New York: Simon and Schuster, 1985. Tedlock's translation of the Popol Vuh is generally considered the definitive English version of the book. Includes a useful introduction with background information, as well as an extensive section of notes.

Websites

Authentic Maya (www.authentic maya.com/maya_religion.htm). A Guatemala-oriented site with many pages that focus on Mayan culture and history. The page titled "Maya Religion" gives a detailed description of the religious beliefs and worship practices of the Maya.

The Metropolitan Museum of Art (www.metmuseum.org/special/Trea sures_of_Sacred_Maya_Kings/maya _more.asp). "Special Exhibitions: Treasures of Ancient Maya Kings." Information on archaeological discoveries in Mayan territory; includes some discussion of mythology.

Yucatán Today (http://Yucatántoday .com/en/homepage). A travel website with historical information about the Yucatán Peninsula. The site includes several traditional Mayan legends and myths.

INDEX

Parker, Joy, 73–74
Pokatok, 60, *61*, 63, *63*, 74, 77
Popol Vuh (Book of Counsel, Mayan Bible)
  creation story from, 46–55, 69, 71, 79, 81
  history of, 47
  source of title, 55
Prometheus, 86, *86*
Proskouriakoff, Tatiana, 19
Pus Master, 68

Q

Quetzalcoatl (Aztec deity), 39, 51, *51*

R

Rain god. *See* Chac
Rain Player (Wisniewski), 77
Religion, 11–12
  art and, 20
  ceremonies, 15
  deities of, 14–15
  worldview of, 12–14
Religious ceremonies, 17–19
Rituals. *See* Religious ceremonies
Rivera, Diego, 49
Royalty, 19–22
  connection between gods and, 21

S

Schele, Linda, 19, 32, 46, 63, 72, 73–74
Scribes, 22–23
Seven Hunahpu, 59–64
Seven Macaw, 65–66, 73–74

Sharer, Robert J., 37, 42
Sky, in Mayan worldview, 13
Star Wars IV (film), 13
Sun god, 30
  Ix Chel as, 39
  See also Kinich Ajaw

T

Tedlock, Dennis, 47, 50, 64
  on Hero Twins, 62, 70, 85
  on punishment of wooden people, 52
Tepew (Heart of Sky, deity), 47
Thompson, J. Eric S., 32, 34
Tikal (city), pyramid at, 24
Toads, *90*
  myth explaining, 89
Tojil (deity), 83–85
Toltex (deity), 36
Two-his-leg, 66

V

Volkmer, Jane Anne, 76, 78

W

Wacah Chan (World tree), 12–13
War god. *See* Buluc Chabtan
Warriors, 22
Weaving/weavers, 34–35, *35*
Wind god. *See* Kukulcan
Wisniewski, David, 77
Wooden people, 50–52
Worldview, 12–14
A Wrinkle in Time (L'Engle), 72

Writing system, 22–23

X

Xaman Ek (deity), 14
Xibalba (underworld), 13
    royalty and, 19–21 *See also*
        Lords of Xibalba
Xikiripat (deity), 14

Y

Yucatán Peninsula, 8
    farming challenges of, 25–27
Yum Kaax (deity), 41

Z

Zotzilaha Chimalman (deity),
    42

PICTURE CREDITS

Stephen Currie has written many books for Lucent, including *African American Literature, Environmentalism in America,* and *Women in the Civil War*. He has also published magazine articles, children's stories, and curriculum materials ranging from kindergarten science to high school mathematics. He lives in New York State.